Praise for *How to Be Good at Performance Appraisals*

"Performance appraisals will always be a daunting challenge for managers. This book provides an excellent practical guide for performance appraisals even though it will always be a controversial subject."

—Mariam Al-Kaabi, Manager, National Development, Qatar Petroleum

"Performance appraisals are one of the most important and frustrating aspects of a manager's job. Dick Grote cuts through the chatter to show us how to make them effective and painless."

—Peter Cappelli, George W. Taylor Professor of Management at the Wharton School and Director of Wharton's Center for Human Resources

"Dick Grote has a terrific way of taking subject matter that has been accepted for many years and making you look at things from a different point of view. His approach is direct and easily understood. If you take the time to think about his ideas and have the courage to use them, I think you will be in a better place."

—David M. Hackett, Senior Vice President, Macy's

"Performance appraisals are demanding and when done right they call for simplicity and courage. It is a relief to discover the real simplicity of performance appraisals described in this book. Learn from it and step into the arena of performance appraisals as a winner!"

—Peter Larsen, Head of HR Operations,
A.P. Moller-Maersk A/S

"Performance appraisals have always been a critical part of a manager's job. Doing them well differentiates the average manager from the outstanding ones. The Millennial workforce—those employees approximately 30 years old and younger—are hungry for performance feedback on a more regular basis than ever before. Being capable of delivering that feedback is, as a result, becoming a key retention tool. If managers cannot do this well, it will result in unnecessary turnover. Dick's philosophy of performance appraisals provides strategies that are easy to understand and execute in order to make meaningful discussions occur. A recommended read!"

—Brian Van Der Weele, Executive Director,
Human Resources, Global Advanced Battery & OEM/OES,
Johnson Controls, Inc.

How to Be Good at
Performance
Appraisals

How to Be Good at
Performance
Appraisals

 Simple

 Effective

 Done Right

Dick Grote

Harvard Business Review Press

Boston, Massachusetts

No part of this publication may be reproduced, stored in, or introduced into a retrieval system or transmitted, in any form or by any means (electronic, mechanical, photocopying, recording, or otherwise), without the prior permission of the publisher. Requests for permission should be directed to permissions@hbsp.harvard.edu or mailed to Permissions, Harvard Business School Publishing, 60 Harvard Way, Boston, Massachusetts 02163.

Library of Congress Cataloging-in-Publication Data

Grote, Dick
    How to be good at performance appraisals : simple, effective, done right / Dick Grote.
        p. cm.
    Includes bibliographical references.
    ISBN 978-1-4221-6228-6 (alk. paper)
    1. Employees—Rating of. 2. Performance standards. I. Title.
    HF5549.5.R3G6416 2011
    658.3′125—dc22

                                2011001317

The paper used in this publication meets the requirements of the American National Standard for Permanence of Paper for Publications and Documents in Libraries and Archives Z39.48-1992.

Contents

Introduction

I received my very first performance appraisal six months after I started to work at General Electric. It was almost brutally frank (and spot-on accurate) in pointing out that I wasn't doing a very good job. It provided the young kid I was then with the wake-up call I needed, telling me dramatically that my school days were over and that tough, rigorous performance expectations were now in place. My boss's straight-between-the-eyes candid feedback—both on the form and in his words—was the jolt I needed to get me to move out of the world of school and into the world of work.

Later I became an HR manager with United Airlines and then with Frito-Lay, where I continued to receive performance appraisals every year from managers who took the process seriously and put a lot of effort into making those appraisals comprehensive and valuable.

Finally, as a consultant specializing exclusively in performance management over the past thirty years, I have helped hundreds of companies create performance appraisal systems that work. I have taught thousands of managers how to successfully do the demanding job of evaluating an individual's performance and then discussing that evaluation with that person.

In all this time, the same questions keep coming up—questions like these:

- How do I do a good job of setting goals? How many goals should I set?

- How do I evaluate a person's behaviors, and how much emphasis should I place on the behavioral part of the person's performance versus the results that she achieves?

- How do I identify a subordinate's development needs?

- How do I determine what the right performance appraisal rating is, and how do I convince the person being evaluated that my rating is correct?

- How do I deliver bad news without killing communication or motivation?

Who This Book Is For

If you supervise people, this book is for you.

Whether or not your company (or *agency* or *firm* or *organization* or *corporation*—I'll use those terms interchangeably) has a formal performance appraisal system, if you have people who report to you, you're a manager (or supervisor or foreman or dean or project head or team leader—whatever the exact term for your job might be). As the manager, you've got to tell the people who report to you what to do and explain how you want it done. You've got to let them know how well they're doing—where they excel, where they're delivering exactly what you expect, and where they need to improve.

If you're a manager, you need to help your people set goals. You need to help them understand the difference between good goals and bad goals. And you need to figure out how well they've done in achieving those goals.

You need to tell your team how you want them to do the job. By "do the job," I'm talking not so much in terms of technical skills and step-by-step instructions, since some of your people probably know more about the technical aspects of their jobs than you do. Rather, I mean that you need to explain how you expect them to act toward others and how you want them to conduct themselves while they're on the company clock.

"Who am I to tell them how to behave?" you might ask. "You're the boss," I'll answer, and people want bosses who make their expectations clear, in terms of both the results they produce and the way they go about producing those results.

You have to evaluate just how well people have done. Have they excelled in their job performance, delivering more than you had expected? Have they performed exactly the way you wanted them to and delivered good, solid performance? Or have there been problems, with some expectations unmet and some results left undelivered?

If your company does have a performance appraisal procedure, then it probably has an appraisal form, and that form probably has a rating scale. In fact, the form may contain rating scales for individual items and then a final rating that sums everything up. How do you use a rating scale well and make meaningful distinctions in individual performance? On a

5-level rating scale, how do you differentiate between someone who's on the high end of the 3 category and someone whose performance has genuinely earned a 4? I will show you how.

Finally, how do you talk with someone who works for you about his performance? Whether the meeting is the fairly formal annual performance review where you go over the appraisal you've written, or the spontaneous coaching and feedback sessions that good managers routinely provide, you'll need to have useful conversations that result in people's doing their jobs better and working more effectively with others on your team.

In other words, this is a book for managers and supervisors—people who have to direct the performance of others and do all the tasks that an organization's performance appraisal process requires. I hope the book is helpful to HR managers, training specialists, and senior executives, but those are not this book's primary audience. My goal for this book is to give supervisors and managers who *aren't* HR experts a solid guide to handling performance appraisal at an Exceeds Expectations level.

What the Book Will Cover

This book will explain how to handle performance appraisal confidently and successfully. No matter what the organization may be, and no matter where it is located—in the United States and Canada, in Europe, or in Southeast Asia or the Middle East—the performance appraisal process used by the great majority of organizations follows the same pattern. At the start of the year managers are expected to meet with each of their direct reports for an hour or so. In this initial meeting they discuss the individual's goals and key job responsibilities. They talk about the behaviors and competencies that are important for the individual's success in getting the job done the way the company wants it done.

After this initial planning meeting, individuals go about doing the job. Managers help them succeed by providing feedback on their performance throughout the year and coaching them to help them do better.

At the end of the year, managers evaluate how well each member of their team has performed and fill out their organization's performance appraisal form. In almost every case, this involves assigning a rating using a rating scale. After the form has been completed and approved, the manager sits down with each individual, reviews the assessment, and explains the reasons behind the ratings. Once this performance appraisal discussion is over, the process begins anew with another meeting to discuss the goals and expectations for the next year.

That's the traditional performance appraisal process. But companies expect managers to do more people-management activities than setting goals, filling out evaluation forms, and reviewing appraisals with subordinates. In the final chapter of the book I will tell you how to handle compensation issues and how to terminate those few people whose performance is so unacceptable that membership in the organization can't be maintained. My goal is not to cover each of these topics exhaustively, but to give you just-in-time, immediately useful suggestions on how to get good at doing each of these additional management responsibilities.

I'll have some unconventional advice for you. I'll warn you against leaning too hard on the SMART acronym for goal setting. I'll recommend that you not ask employees to complete a self-appraisal. And I'll tell you why the time-honored "sandwich approach" to conducting appraisal discussions—in which the manager combines some feedback on the employee's strengths and successes with a review of the areas where improvement is needed—is a really bad idea.

Simple, Effective, Done Right

Finally, let me tell you frankly that performance appraisal is strenuous and demanding. It's the Olympic Games of management. And no matter how solid my advice may be or how skilled you may be as a manager, performance appraisal will always be difficult. I know that some people think that if somehow we get the forms, the procedures, the timing, and the training right, then performance appraisal will be easy.

That's a myth. No matter how good a job we do at improving forms and policies, training and skills, performance appraisal will never be comfortable and routine. It will always be difficult because performance appraisal requires people in supervisory jobs to do something they have always been told not to do—be judgmental of others. Performance appraisal requires managers to stand in judgment of each person on their team, to evaluate just how well or how poorly they have performed, and then to review that assessment face to face. Very few people enjoy having their performance analyzed, documented, and discussed. It's one of the hardest things we ask people in leadership positions to do.

There's no way to make that job easy. But we can make it workable. And providing workable, tested, practical information is my goal for this book. My objective is to make performance appraisal and all of the activities connected with this procedure less taxing than they need to be.

Many of the problems presented by performance appraisal result from excessively complicated forms, cumbersome policies, and training that isn't practical. Frankly, performance appraisal doesn't have to be that difficult. In almost every organization I have worked with, the performance appraisal process can be simplified, the form shortened, and the administrative burden reduced, without any loss in the quality of the information provided to either the company or the individual. It is possible to keep it simple, make it effective, and do it right. And it's possible for individual managers to do this, without the need for corporate permission or consent. Everything I recommend is simply good management practice.

Of course, if a company mandates that a long and complicated form be used and insists that complex procedures be followed, the individual manager is limited in what he or she can do to change this. But most organizations don't insist, for example, that a dozen goals be set. They simply include a section on goal setting in the appraisal form. If a company provides a dozen or more competencies against which each person's performance must be evaluated, there's nothing that prevents the manager from telling each of his subordinates at the start of the year which two or three of those competencies will make the biggest impact—and carry the greatest weight when performance appraisal time rolls around.

Performance appraisal, done right, can produce the same powerful and beneficial results for everyone in an organization that it did for me at the start of my career. The techniques and skills that I'll give you in this book, combined with your courage to put them to use, will benefit you, your organization, and every one of your subordinates who look to you for leadership.

Chapter 1

Why Bother with Performance Appraisal?

In my e-mail inbox this morning was a newsletter that a colleague writes monthly with some of his musings. One of them: "Before someone can understand *how* effectively, they usually need to know *what* and *why* first." That makes sense. So let's start by looking at exactly what performance appraisal is and why we do it, and then get a sense of how most companies handle the basic elements of performance appraisal—what the common and uncommon performance appraisal practices are.

What Is a Performance Appraisal?

One of the most basic causes of performance appraisal failure is that so few people understand just what a performance appraisal is. Listen up: *A performance appraisal is a formal record of a manager's opinion of the quality of an employee's work.*

The operant word here is *opinion.* Performance appraisal requires a manager to render his opinion about exactly how well an individual performed. It is not a document that can be empirically tested and proven. It is not the end product of a negotiation between the manager and the individual. It is a record of the manager's judgment about exactly how good a job Joe or Jane has done over the past twelve months.

As long as that judgment is based on the manager's honest assessment of how well the job has been done and is uncolored by personal prejudices and biases, the performance appraisal is virtually immune from a disgruntled employee's legal challenge. The notion that delivering an honest but negative performance appraisal will lead to an appearance on the witness stand in a discrimination lawsuit is an unfounded myth. Courts have consistently upheld the right of organizations to make business- and employment-related decisions based on managers' opinions as recorded in performance appraisals, even when those opinions are based only on the manager's observations, judgment, and experience without provable, quantifiable data to support them. This deference by the courts to employers has been stated as the *business judgment rule* and has been acknowledged by the courts plainly: "We do not assume the role of a 'super-personnel department,' assessing the merits or even the rationality of employers' nondiscriminatory business decisions."[1] Again, the appraisal is a record of a manager's opinion. If the employee and the manager disagree about that opinion, the manager wins.

Why Do Performance Appraisal?

Performance appraisal *is* important. It serves a vital and irreplaceable function. Consider this: Every person who works for an organization wants the answers to two questions: (1) What do you expect of me? and (2) How am I doing at meeting your expectations? The first question is answered at the start of the year, when managers discuss goals, expected behaviors, and key job responsibilities with each member of the team. The second question is answered at the end of the year when managers evaluate each individual's performance and then discuss that evaluation with the employee.

Equally important, an effective performance appraisal system is the primary mechanism that allows organizations to make critically important decisions correctly. Decisions like:

- How should rewards be allocated? Who should get a big raise, and who should get nothing at all?

- When a vacancy arises, who should be tapped for promotion? Do we have excellent candidates already ready and waiting, or do we have to go outside to get the talent we need?

- What's the depth of our talent pool? Do we have the people we need to meet the demands of the future?

- What is the relative strength of talent across our organization? Are there pockets of excellence and pockets of mediocrity within the company?

- Who are our best performers, the people who do outstanding work in their present positions with the

potential to take on more demanding roles? Do we have
retention strategies in place to make sure that they
don't leave us?

- Who are our worst performers, and what do we need to
  do about them? Which ones can we salvage? Which ones
  should we cut loose?

If the performance appraisal system isn't intelligently
designed and skillfully used, the answers to these critical questions may of course be wrong. Worse, the questions won't even
be asked, and the organization will stumble toward its strategic goals without knowing whether it has the talent it needs to
assure their achievement.

Common Practices in Performance Appraisal

If you looked over the performance appraisal forms from a few
dozen of America's largest organizations, your immediate reaction might be that the forms all look different and have nothing
in common. But underlying the surface differences are some
striking similarities in the way companies approach the business of performance appraisal.

Performance appraisal itself is common. First, the fact is
that almost all companies have performance appraisal systems.
The larger the organization, the higher the probability that it
will have a formal procedure that requires that goals and objectives be set at the start of the year, that coaching and feedback
be provided during the year, and that an assessment of the individual's performance and a discussion of that assessment be
conducted at the end of the year.

Goal setting. Goal setting is a prime component in virtually all performance appraisal systems. Setting goals, as we'll see later, works. A study by Distinguished Professor Edward E. Lawler III of the University of Southern California and Michael McDermott of Capital One found that more than four out of five organizations use performance-driven goals.[2]

Rating scales. In most cases, an overall performance rating is provided using a 5-level rating scale. We'll discuss using a rating scale in chapter 7, but for now it's worth noting that almost all companies use a rating scale, that most use a 5-level rating scale, and that the use of a 5-level scale is increasing.

Competencies. The use of competencies is also a common practice. Eighty-three percent of organizations today have identified the behavioral expectations for organization members, either company-wide or for specific types of jobs. Studies have found that using competencies drives better performance and that organizations that make excellent use of competencies are four times more likely to have a performance-driven culture.[3]

Behaviors and results. Human performance is a function of two components—behaviors (how the person goes about doing the job) and results (what the person accomplishes). These two dimensions of job performance are loosely correlated. It's possible for an individual to produce great results with poor behaviors (for example, the used car salesman who always makes his quota but does so by lying to customers, rolling back odometers, and stealing other salesmen's leads). It's equally possible to have an individual whose behaviors are sterling but who simply doesn't accomplish much. Most appraisal procedures call for evaluating people's performance in terms of both how they do their jobs and what they get done.

Other common practices used by a majority of companies in their performance appraisal systems include incorporating development planning into the overall performance appraisal process; requiring that both the performance appraisal document and the rating determined by a manager be reviewed by at least one higher-level individual before the appraisal is reviewed with the employee and becomes official; and providing a fairly tight linkage between a person's performance appraisal rating and the size of his or her merit increase.

Finally, what is common in performance appraisal is a fairly universal feeling among all system users—appraisers, appraisees, senior executives, and HR professionals—that we still have a ways to go before we've got it right. Depending on the study, the primary areas that fall short are managers' ability to coach subordinates; the linkage between performance appraisal and other HR systems like development planning, compensation, and succession planning; and the alignment between performance appraisal and business strategy.

What's Not So Common in Performance Appraisal?

There are several practices that have been proven to have a positive impact on human performance and on increasing the effectiveness of performance appraisal, but aren't used all that much, in spite of the benefits they provide.

Calibration. While using calibration sessions to increase appraisal accuracy is far from universal, it's a technique that is rapidly gaining popularity. Calibration sessions are meetings in which managers who supervise comparable positions discuss in advance the ratings they are planning to give each of their staff members. The planned appraisal ratings are discussed, debated, and revised to assure that one manager's Meets Expectations represents the same quality of performance as the same rating from any other manager, and that a level playing field exists throughout the department or company.

Calibration sessions were developed only about a decade ago, but in that time their use has been growing rapidly. Today more than half of all major organizations have incorporated some form of calibration process into their performance appraisal procedures.

Assessing how well managers do appraisals. Another high-payoff/infrequently used practice evaluates managers on how well they execute their performance management responsibilities. We know that "what gets measured, gets done." Therefore, an easy way to increase the effectiveness of companies' performance appraisal procedures is to add an assessment item on every managerial appraisal form that asks the manager's boss to rate how good a job the manager did in writing his performance appraisals of his team members. While this is an obvious and highly workable quick fix, less than a quarter of all companies actually evaluate managers on how well they execute their performance management responsibilities.

Rapid termination of low performers. Another uncommon practice is the direct termination of people who earn the lowest appraisal rating. Academic research has clearly demonstrated that identifying the poorest-performing 10 percent of an organization's employees, terminating them, and replacing them with higher-performing replacements significantly improves the quality of the workforce.[4]

But rarely do companies routinely terminate those who end up at the bottom of the rating scale.

Greater use of 360-degree feedback. Another fairly familiar tool that is seldom used in performance appraisals is 360-degree feedback. Less than half of all organizations make use of formal 360-degree programs, and those that do use 360-degree feedback almost exclusively for developmental purposes. Though 360-degree data may shed some light on the quality of a person's performance in the behavioral dimension of job performance, it's rare for 360-degree feedback results to be used in performance appraisal.

Training. Frequency of training varies widely. It's fairly common for appraisers to be given some form of training in the various elements of performance appraisal. It's rare for employees—appraisal recipients—to get any training or orientation about how the overall process works or how they can benefit from a performance appraisal discussion, set goals, determine their key job responsibilities, conduct a self-appraisal, or do almost any of the other chores involved in the performance appraisal process. Training has a very high correlation with system effectiveness, and companies with well-developed systems are usually also the ones that have a high commitment to training.

Web-based appraisal systems. Finally, although the use of Web-based performance appraisal systems is growing, it is doing so much more slowly than was expected when these systems were first developed and marketed to organizations in the late 1990s. Estimates of the percentage of large organizations that have moved to a fully Web-based performance appraisal process range between 40 and 50 percent, although a significant number of these are companies that have simply turned their paper-based system into an online form, as opposed to purchasing a ready-made product from an outside vendor.

Web-based systems do offer significant benefits in easing administrative burdens. However, they also add a significant level of complexity, particularly with the growing trend by vendors to offer not just a performance appraisal product, but a whole suite of software products that are claimed to integrate such processes as succession planning, leadership development, learning management, competency development, and other pieces of the whole talent management process. While these systems hold promise for easing the administrative burden through automation, too often they add to that burden by including every bell and whistle that can easily be tacked on. The expectations of a decade ago that virtually all companies would quickly move to Web-based appraisal systems have proven to be highly inflated.

Putting It All Together

In spite of the many criticisms of performance appraisal, the process serves a vital business purpose by providing the data that organizations and their leaders need to make important decisions. The performance appraisal process also allows managers to meet their ethical obligation to let every one of their staffers know exactly what is expected of them and how they're doing in meeting those expectations. Performance appraisal and annual budgeting are probably the two most commonly used management procedures.

Virtually every performance appraisal system has some common features:

- A goal-setting component.
- The inclusion of competencies, both company-wide and for specific types of jobs.
- A rating scale to indicate a final assessment of performance.
- The use of a 5-level scale.
- A development planning component.
- A requirement that both the appraisal and the rating be reviewed by at least one higher-level individual and/or HR before the appraisal becomes official.
- A tight linkage between the performance appraisal rating and compensation.

The following high-payoff techniques are used less often:

- Calibration sessions to help assure a common yardstick in evaluating people's performance (although the use of calibration sessions grows every year).
- Assessing how well managers do their job of appraising performance.
- Routinely terminating low performers.

- Using 360-degree feedback results as a data source for evaluating performance.

- Universal training (particularly for appraisees).

- The use of externally provided Web-based systems.

Chapter 2

Goal Setting

There's a wonderful urban myth about the power of goal setting. According to a host of motivational speakers and self-help gurus, back in 1953 researchers surveyed Yale's graduating seniors to determine how many of them had specific written goals for their future. The answer: 3 percent. Twenty years later, researchers polled the surviving members of the class of 1953 and found that the 3 percent with goals had accumulated more personal financial wealth than the other 97 percent of the class combined!

It's a terrific story, and a convincing tribute to the power of goal setting—"a vivid Ivy League success story that documents the cause-and-effect relationship between goals and personal success," writer Lawrence Tabak explains in relating and debunking the story. Turns out, there's not a word of truth in it.[1]

But this bogus example doesn't cancel out the overwhelming research-based data that demonstrates that goal setting in an organizational context does have a powerful positive influence on performance and motivation.

What the Research Says

A few years ago professors Edwin A. Locke and Gary P. Latham, the two most-recognized academic researchers on goal setting, wrote an article that summarized their thirty-five years of research in this area.[2] What did they find?

- Setting specific, difficult goals consistently leads to higher performance than just urging people to do their best.

- Goals are energizing. High goals generate greater effort than low goals, and the highest or most difficult goals produce the greatest levels of effort and performance.

- Tight deadlines lead to a more rapid work pace than loose deadlines.

- Making a public commitment to a goal enhances personal commitment.

- Whether the goal is set by mutual agreement or by the boss doesn't make a big difference in goal achievement.

It appears to be an open-and-shut case. Set specific, difficult goals with tight deadlines and let everyone know what they are. Don't be too concerned about whether the goal is jointly set by the individual together with the manager, or whether the boss just hands the subordinate the list of goals he expects the subordinate to achieve by a tough due date. Let everybody know what your goals are. The predictable result: increased effort, persistence, and performance.

But Can We Be Too Goal Focused?

Others caution against too much of a good thing. There are very real problems with goal setting, according to Professor Lisa Ordoñez and her colleagues in their "Goals Gone Wild" critique of overprescribing goal setting as a motivational and performance-enhancement tool. They explain that while goals do focus people's attention, they may focus it so narrowly that people overlook other important features of a task.[3] To make their point, they reference a clever and well-known video that demonstrates selective attention and inattentional blindness. Viewers watch a group of people passing basketballs and are told to count the number of passes made by the team wearing white shirts. Focusing entirely on the assigned task, most people watching the video fail to notice the tall man dressed in a black gorilla suit who walks into the middle of the group, pounds his chest a few times, and then walks off.[4] "Intense concentration on the counting task causes people to overlook a striking element of their visual world," they point out.[5]

Goal setting causes people to narrow their focus, concentrating exclusively on goal attainment and ignoring important issues that appear to be unrelated to goal achievement. Another illustration from the authors of "Goals Gone Wild" is that of a university department that bases tenure decisions primarily on the number of papers that professors publish. While this goal will motivate professors to achieve the narrow goal of publishing papers, other important aspects of the job—like teaching, counseling students, serving on faculty committees, advising student groups, and so forth—may suffer. The authors caution: "Consistent with the classic notion that you get what you reward, goal setting may cause people to ignore important dimensions of performance that are not specified by the goal setting system."[6]

There's also a question about the dangers of setting goals that are excessively challenging. Professor Ordoñez and her colleagues make a case that the benefits of setting high goals may be offset by the undesired negative results such stretch goals are likely to generate:

> *Proponents of goal setting claim that a positive linear relationship exists between the difficulty of a goal and employee performance. Specifically, they argue that goals should be set at the most challenging level possible to inspire effort, commitment, and performance—but not so challenging that employees see no point in trying. This logic makes intuitive sense, yet stretch goals also caused serious side effects: Shifting risk attitudes, promoting unethical behavior, and triggering the psychological costs of goal failure.[7]*

The authors contend that faced with a seemingly overwhelming goal, employees are more likely to engage in unethical behaviors (like a lawyer's double-billing clients), take on unwise risks (like lending money for mortgages knowing that the borrower is unlikely to be able to repay), and cheat by reporting that a missed goal was achieved (like reporting sales calls that were never made).

While the efficacy of goal setting is firmly established, the risks and downsides are real too. What both camps miss is that in organizations, goals and goal setting are simply one important part of the job as a whole. They are not the job in its entirety. Goal-setting researchers focus narrowly on the impact of setting goals on the achievement of a single task. When only one task is to be achieved, there's no question that specific, challenging goals will result in increased performance.

But jobs are much more than a bunch of individual tasks. Many important aspects of job performance are unsuitable targets for goal setting, like helping a colleague caught in a last-minute crisis, coaching a junior member of the staff, helping a newcomer get off to a good start, or referring a friend who's a great match for a job that the company has been trying unsuccessfully to fill. These "citizenship behaviors" aren't amenable to formalized goal setting, but they make for a workplace that is likely to be highly engaged and committed to the company's success.

Making Goal Setting Work

As long as we understand that goal setting has some very real limitations, setting appropriate goals is a vital part of the performance appraisal process. Earlier, I defined *performance* as a combination of two factors: behaviors and results. Goal setting is most appropriate in the *results* dimension of the job. Goals provide employees with direction on where their efforts should be placed, identify the small number of vital outcomes they are expected to produce, and help them focus their efforts on accomplishing those results that will have the highest benefit to the organization—without unduly sacrificing all the other components of the job that the manager and the organization expect from the individual.

So in spite of all the real risks and pitfalls, goal setting remains a powerful tool for enhancing performance and motivation. But while the effectiveness of goal setting done right is unarguable, one of the challenges is determining the areas where goals need to be set. Where should someone look to find places where setting a wise goal and achieving it would have a significant impact on performance and business success?

Sources of Goals

Cheaper/faster/better is the first area to explore. Consider the parts of the individual's job where the person spends the most time or the areas where the results produced have the biggest impact on the department's or the company's success. How can expenses be reduced? Or less time spent while delivering the same level of quality? Or performance improved?

For those in professional individual contributor or leadership jobs, seeking ways to perform cheaper/faster/better should be a standard and routine part of the job, not a special item that is worth a separate goal. But for jobs in the administrative or support sectors, asking people to look for ways to do their jobs cheaper/faster/better can be a valuable starting place for finding meaningful goals.

Here are other areas that can be explored as valuable sources of goals:

Company mission statement/vision and values

Goals from previous review period

Job description

Comments and suggestions from previous performance appraisals

Critical job responsibilities

Your boss's objectives and items listed on executives'
Balanced Scorecards

Division/department plans and strategies

Discussions with colleagues/more senior managers/
internal clients/customers

The Goals Grid

A useful technique for identifying important goals whose
achievement will have a significant beneficial impact on the organization is the Goals Grid, a technique developed by consultant and researcher Fred Nickols.[8]

Begin by asking four questions:

1. What do you want that you don't have? (*Achieve*)

2. What do you want that you already have? (*Preserve*)

3. What don't you have that you don't want? (*Avoid*)

4. What do you have now that you don't want? (*Eliminate*)

The answers to those four questions form the basis of the
Goals Grid, shown in figure 2-1.

The Goals Grid is a useful tool, both to identify areas where
goals should be set and to achieve goal clarity. It prompts us to
think about our goals in an organized fashion, from four different perspectives. It is beneficial to consciously think through
our objectives, not just in terms of what we want to *achieve* but
also in terms of what we want to *preserve*, what we wish to
avoid, and what we wish to *eliminate*.

FIGURE 2-1

The Goals Grid

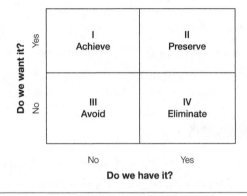

Another benefit of using the Goals Grid is that it forces us to expand our thinking beyond a limited focus on only what we want to achieve. By thinking of those things that we want to protect, avoid, and eliminate, we are more likely to set goals that will have a significant impact on organization success. Consider this: it may be that all of your goals cluster in the Eliminate quadrant. Does this suggest a preoccupation with the negative side of things, or are you just caught up in a bad situation? Suppose all of your objectives are equally divided between the Preserve and Avoid quadrants. Could this indicate an unwillingness to take risks?

Another useful exercise is to think about potential conflicts between your objectives and someone else's objectives. Who might wish to avoid what you're trying to achieve? Who might wish to preserve what you're trying to eliminate? Turn those same questions around: Who might gain from achieving what you're trying to avoid? Who might profit from eliminating what you're striving to preserve?

Some Examples of Well-Set Goals

Following are examples of goals in three different types of jobs—one each in the professional/technical, managerial/supervisory, and administrative job families—that seem to be wisely set, along with some anticipated outcomes and measures for each. They are good illustrations of goals that, if achieved, are likely to require some stretch on the part of the performer, are measurable, and will have a beneficial impact on the performer's organization.

Registered Nurse

Goal 1: Develop and conduct an in-service education program on dealing effectively with the Cambodian patient/family.

> *Anticipated outcomes and measures:* Involve the Cambodian resource center staff; receive high evaluations from participants; complete by January 1.

Goal 2: Obtain ACLS licensure.

> *Anticipated outcomes and measures:* Obtain licensure by October 15.

Operations Manager

Goal 1: Develop the internal CAD system into a marketable product (a shared goal with the marketing manager).

> *Anticipated outcomes and measures:* Cost to bring the CAD system to market; quality of competitive analysis; acceptance by two customers by March 31.

Goal 2: Identify and install a replacement for the Cryo-techtonics feeder.

Anticipated outcomes and measures: Feeder up and running by June 30; no significant downtime; reasonable overtime usage.

Goal 3: Significantly upgrade the talent pool in the operations division.

Anticipated outcomes and measures: Greater number of high-potential employees identified in the annual succession planning process; no high-potential employees resigning from the company; termination of marginal performers with little disruption or legal problems.

Administrative Assistant/Secretary

Goal 1: Serve effectively on the employee benefits upgrade task force.

Anticipated outcomes and measures: Complete review and recommendations to senior management committee by end of third quarter; recommendations accepted by management.

Goal 2: Analyze effectiveness of existing travel agency and other travel suppliers and recommend any changes required.

Anticipated outcomes and measures: Recommendation to retain or replace existing travel agency made by June 1; step-by-step transition plan created (if new agency is chosen); reduced travel costs; fewer complaints about bad service from company employees.

Goal 3: Develop skills necessary to provide graphics support to department.

Anticipated outcomes and measures: Choose and learn a graphics package; evaluate whether attending an outside training program is cost effective; provide graphics services to department members that please them.

Some key points: notice that the last goal isn't stated as "Attend a training program on designing graphics." Training is a mechanism, a system input, a means to get to what is really important—the ability to provide graphics support to the department. Whether the administrative assistant develops the skills needed to provide effective graphics support by reading a book, by getting coaching from her cousin who's a graphics professional, or just by playing with the software makes no difference. The goal will have been accomplished. Note also that one of the success measures is to "provide graphics services to department members that please them." There is no feasible way to quantify the pleasure level of department members, but their reactions can be assessed just by asking them how they feel.

Also, note that the goal of the operations manager to develop the internal CAD system into a marketable product is a shared goal with the marketing manager. If achieving a goal will be the responsibility of more than one person, it's important for both of them to include that goal in their performance plan. Finally, in the "anticipated outcomes and measures" of some of the operations manager's goals, there are statements like "reasonable overtime usage" and "little disruption." Who's to judge whether the overtime usage is reasonable or the termination of marginal performers created little disruption? The operations manager's boss, that's who, when appraisal time rolls around. But when the goal is set at the beginning of the performance period, there's no way to specify precisely what "reasonable" or "little" will actually turn out to be.

Six Bad Ideas in Goal Setting

Several popular goal-setting techniques turn out to be generally unproductive in practice: using the SMART acronym for goal setting, cascading goals from a higher level, indicating percentage weights for goals, setting numerous goals, using the Balanced Scorecard throughout the organization, and setting goals in accordance with people's capabilities.

Bad Idea #1—SMART Goals

If a company provides managers with performance appraisal training, in almost every case there will be a unit explaining SMART goals. By now, almost everyone who works for an organization is familiar with the hackneyed SMART acronym for setting goals: goals must be Specific, Measurable, Attainable, Realistic, and Time-bound.

What's wrong with SMART goals? First, in a great many organizations the discussion of goal setting never goes any further than telling managers to set goals and make sure that they meet the SMART test. But managers aren't told where they should look for goals, how to determine whether their goals are appropriate and genuinely important, or how to make sure there's some congruity between the goals that individuals set and the business strategy of the department or the organization as a whole.

Another problem is that while the SMART test may be a useful mechanism for making sure that a goal statement has been phrased correctly (in the same way that a spell-checker is a useful mechanism by flagging any misspelled words in a document), it doesn't help at all in determining whether the goal itself is a good idea. In other words, a goal can be SMART without being wise. All a spell-checker can do is tell you whether you've misspelled any words. It can't help you determine whether what you've written is any good; it can't distinguish between the Declaration of Independence and *Mein Kampf.*

For example, consider the goal statement announced by President John F. Kennedy on May 25, 1961:

> *I believe that this nation should commit itself to achieving the goal, before this decade is out, of landing a man on the moon, and returning him safely to the earth.*

How does Kennedy's goal statement stack up against the SMART test? Remarkably well. It's certainly specific and time-bound, and it's easily measurable. Realistic and attainable? While there are still a few cranks who contend that the first moon landing was actually filmed on a Warner Brothers back lot, the fact is that on July 21, 1969, Neil Armstrong became the first man to set foot on the moon, stepping onto the moon's surface in the Sea of Tranquility at 0256 GMT.

Kennedy's goal clearly was SMART. But was it wise?

The man-on-the-moon program provided great benefits: a huge psychological boost in the race for space with the Russians, the creation of lots of jobs, an increased focus on science and technology, a couple of moon rocks, and the development of Velcro fasteners and Tang powdered orange juice substitute.

But it also cost a huge amount—the best estimate is about $170 billion. For that amount of money we could have built several universities the size of the University of Illinois, or provided a 1,200-square-foot house for every American living under the poverty line. Would these have been better investments than shoveling $170 billion into a rocket ship and blasting it into outer space?

Nobody knows, because the question wasn't asked. Once the goal had been set by the president and enthusiastically taken up by Congress in the optimistic early 1960s, nobody bothered to question whether there were better ways of spending this colossal amount of money. Landing a man on the moon was SMART. Nobody asked whether it was wise.

The best use for the SMART test is exactly that—as a test of somewhat minor importance to make sure that an individual's final goal statements are appropriately stated. But SMART can't tell you whether a goal should actually be set.

The biggest problem with using the SMART test as the exclusive criterion for whether goals are properly set is that it encourages the setting of low goals. No one is going to set goals that are not attainable or realistic, but setting goals that are sure to be achieved violates one of the main findings of Locke and Latham's thirty-five-year study of what makes goal setting effective: "The highest or most difficult goals produced the greatest levels of effort and performance."[9] If they abide by the SMART test's counsel, every individual will stay within his comfort zone and set only those goals that are sure winners.

The best course of action may be to dump the SMART test and insist that people set wise goals that truly test the limits of their capabilities.

Bad Idea #2—Cascading Goals

A piece of frequently offered advice on goal setting is that goals should cascade down from the top of the organization. The president starts by setting her goals. The vice presidents then set their goals to support the achievement of the president's objectives. Then the directors determine their goals based on the ones the VPs have set, followed in turn by the managers, then by the supervisors, and finally by those at the bottom of the organizational food chain.

Of course, the goals of a subordinate at any level in the organization should not conflict with the goals set by his or her manager, and should support the achievement of the boss's and company's objectives. Too often, however, the cascading process is followed as a rigid, lock-step procedure in which no one can begin to set goals until those of the immediate supervisor have been determined and provided to those below. Worse, organizations that insist on the cascading of goals often directly or unintentionally send the message that all of the subordinate's goals need to link directly to the goals of the immediate supervisor.

I saw this cascading-goals problem arise a few years ago at CARE, the humanitarian organization fighting global poverty. At that time CARE followed a rigid procedure that provided that before any country director could set his or her goals, the goals of the area director had to be set and communicated first. While this seemed to be a logical approach, the area director (for Africa, for example) was often called away to support a particular crisis in another part of the world where CARE's help was vitally needed. The consequence was that goal setting ground to a halt while people waited for the area director to return and complete her goal-setting task.

The solution is to free the goal-setting process from the rigid requirement that individual goals must be tightly linked to the supervisor's goals and limited to the areas in which the supervisor or the organization has set goals. The goals set by one's immediate supervisor represent an important source of information about where a person might logically set her own goals, but should never limit the goal setting done by the individual. Every job has areas in which the individual performer can work to support the goals of her boss. However, every job also has elements where the individual's work is not directly related to the boss's goals but still supports the organization's overall business strategy. Don't let goal setting get hung up by rigidly insisting that all goals must neatly cascade from above.

Bad Idea #3—Requiring Percentage Weights for Goals

At one of America's largest intelligence agencies, as in a great many other organizations, not only are goals the dominant component of the performance appraisal system, but individuals and their supervisors are required to indicate a percentage weight for each goal, with the minimum weight for any goal being 5 percent.

Letting people know that some goals are more important than others is a good idea, but assigning percentage weights to goals is a bad idea, for several reasons. First, it's impossible to accurately identify the relative importance of goals at a 5 percent level of granularity. Should one particular goal be assessed as reflecting 20 percent of the total weight for all goals, or should it be 25 percent? And from which other goal should the additional 5 percent be taken? This argument isn't productive, and it is even less productive in organizations that don't limit the percentage weight at all. In these organizations, arguments can arise about whether a particular goal should be weighted at 16 percent or 18 percent. That's unproductive.

Allowing the percentage weighting of goals creates a more serious problem later in the performance appraisal process. If each goal is assigned a percentage weight, then appraisers are likely to turn the assessment of human performance into the solving of an arithmetic problem. Given a percentage weight assigned to each goal, and a 5-level rating scale, appraisers are tempted (or even instructed) to multiply the percentage weight of the goal times the numerical score they've assigned to determine the assessment rating for that item. When this first chore is done and the scores for each item have been determined, they are then to add all the individual ratings and divide by the total number of items to compute a mean score, which will then provide the final performance appraisal rating, out to one or two decimal points. This approach may be mathematically precise, but it's nonsense. Performance appraisal isn't a matter of mathematical precision. It's a matter of managerial judgment, as we'll discuss in chapter 6.

Don't assign percentage weights. Don't try to get any more granular than indicating High, Medium, and Low or listing goals in the approximate order of importance to indicate the relative degree of significance of each goal compared with the others.

Bad Idea #4—Setting Numerous Goals

There's an almost universal concurrence that one of the biggest problems with goal setting is that people set too many. HR expert Kris Dunn observes that humans are stackers and hoarders. Left to our own devices, we'll hoard things because we don't want to make decisions about what's most important. But stacking and hoarding is poison when it comes to setting performance goals. If you give a person two goals, he'll probably make progress toward accomplishing both, given talent and resources. Make it five goals and he'll make progress toward two or three. More than five? Little is likely to be accomplished on any, since there's too much to focus on and any individual goal is by itself relatively unimportant.[10]

Limit the number of goals to three or at most four that are tough, specific, and have a significant impact on the success of the department or the business as a whole. If a person is able to meet all the expectations of her position that would be detailed in a well-written job description, and in addition can achieve two or three significant goals in the course of a twelve-month period, that person's had a good year.

Bad Idea #5—Using the Balanced Scorecard Throughout the Organization

The Balanced Scorecard is a management tool developed by Robert Kaplan and David Norton. The Balanced Scorecard was developed to broaden the focus of senior executives beyond traditional financial measures to include the customer perspective, the internal processes perspective, and the learning and growth perspective:

- **Financial perspective:** Traditional measures include economic value added, operating income, and return on capital employed.

- **Customer perspective:** Examples of these measures are customer satisfaction scores, customer growth, customer retention, and market share.

- **Business process perspective:** For business processes such as procurement, supply chain management, production, and order fulfillment, measures might be cost, quality, and processing time required.

- **Learning and growth perspective:** Measures in this area might include employee retention, time to hire, and loss of critical talent.

The use of the formal Balanced Scorecard procedure is most appropriate at senior executive levels. However, many organizations expand the use of the Balanced Scorecard to jobs lower in the organization, requiring that everyone set goals in accordance with the Balanced Scorecard framework. Mandating for all jobs the use of a tool that was originally designed for the executive level of the organization doesn't work well, since the perspective of people in lower-level jobs is more narrowly focused. It's certainly helpful for everyone in the organization to see the Balanced Scorecards developed by the executive team and to use them as guidelines for the areas in which they should consider setting goals. But forcing the rigid application of the Balanced Scorecard throughout the organization hinders rather than helps goal setting.

Bad Idea #6—Setting Goals Based on Individuals' Capabilities Rather Than on Business Needs

A questionable piece of management advice recommends that managers take the abilities of their subordinates into account when setting each person's goals. Goal setting, argue Professor Lisa Ordoñez and her colleagues, can be problematic when the same goal is applied to many different people: "Given the variability of performance on any given task, any standard goal set for a group of people will vary in difficulty for individual members; thus, the goal will simultaneously be too easy for some and too difficult for others. Conversely, idiosyncratically tailoring goals to each individual can lead to charges of unfairness."[11] In simpler words, if a manager assigns the same goal to everyone on the team, he may be perceived as foolish since some people will be able to far exceed the results specified while others will be unable to achieve them. But if he tailors the goal to correspond with each person's capability level, he'll be seen as unfair for setting the goals of some people higher than those assigned to others. Worse, he may be seen as discriminatory if he lets some people slide by with a low goal while others are held to a higher standard.

Consider a manager with three subordinates, all holding similar positions. We'll call them Peter, Paul, and Mary. Peter's the best of the bunch, a talented and highly motivated future CEO. Paul's a good solid citizen, a Steady Eddie who always delivers reliable, meets-expectations, fully successful performance. Mary is the runt of the litter. Lightly skilled and unmotivated, she produces just enough to get by. Following the bad advice that he took away from his company's Management 101 training program about taking the capabilities of one's subordinates into account in setting goals, the manager assigns Peter a goal of 75, Paul a goal of 65, and Mary a goal of 55.

When performance appraisal time rolls around, the manager discovers that Peter has achieved only 73. Paul—as could be predicted—delivers the expected 65. And Mary, surprisingly, ends up achieving 57. Which one has exceeded expectations? It's Mary, who is by far the poorest performer.

And what's the manager to do now, since the compensation system dictates a 3 percent raise to all those who have exceeded expectations, 2 percent to those who have achieved expectations, and nothing for those in the Fails to Meet category? Worse, what does he do when a reduction in force is required and he's told to cut loose anyone who ended up in the bottom rating category?

The correct solution is to set goals based on the needs of the business and not on the capability of the individuals. If the job level and pay and experience of various people is reasonably comparable, the same expectations should be set for each. In our example, the appropriate target for all three would be 75. Peter will accept it and go about delivering the results. Paul will require some coaching and guidance to make it up to the higher standard. And Mary will complain that the manager is setting her up for failure, knowing full well that she's not capable of delivering 75. The manager's response is that 75 is what the job requires. If she's incapable of performing at that level, then she needs to find another job where the expectations are lower.

———————————

In sum, goal setting works. The conclusions of Latham and Locke and those of Lawler and McDermott are well founded, as are the concerns of Professor Ordoñez and her colleagues. What is important in goal setting is to refrain from setting too many goals, avoid using percentage weights, avoid forcing the use of the Balanced Scorecard and cascading goals, and—perhaps most important—to avoid blindly applying the SMART test, thinking that it ensures the goal-setting job is done. On the other hand, effective goal setting involves looking beyond just what you want to achieve to assess those things that you need to avoid, preserve, or eliminate; going beyond cheaper/faster/better; exploring many sources to make sure that every area where a significant goal might be set has been considered; and finding reasonably easy-to-measure outcomes that will provide a solid indication of the extent to which the goal has been achieved.

Principles to Remember

DO

✓ Set specific, difficult goals with tight deadlines.

✓ Let everyone know what your goals are.

✓ Use the SMART test only to check whether goals are well written, not to determine whether they're wise.

DON'T

✓ Be too concerned whether the goal is employee-set or boss-imposed.

✓ Assign percentage weights to goals.

✓ Set goals that encourage unwise risk taking or inappropriate behaviors.

Chapter 3

Determining Key Job Responsibilities

Not every part of a job is covered in the goals that an individual sets. A person's goals represent the two to four major achievements that he or she is going to strive to attain, while still executing all of the other responsibilities required of someone holding the position. Goals describe what one is going to do *in addition to* meeting one's job description responsibilities. But what are those "job description responsibilities"?

Unfortunately, in most cases the job description itself doesn't provide much help. Job descriptions tend to be written generally and are designed to serve many different purposes. It's unlikely that a job description will mirror precisely the exact responsibilities of someone who is assigned to that position.

This is particularly true for those jobs where many people hold the same title, like financial analyst, administrative assistant, or IT support technician. The actual duties and responsibilities of an admin or IT tech working in one department are likely to vary quite a bit from those of someone with the same title working in a different department. It's therefore unlikely that this type of generic job description will describe the actual duties and responsibilities expected of one particular individual so well that the words can be lifted verbatim for use in a performance appraisal. The job description is a *starting point* for figuring out an individual's key job responsibilities, not the final answer.

KRAs and KPIs

KRA and KPI are two confusing acronyms for an approach commonly recommended for identifying a person's major job responsibilities. KRA stands for *key result areas*; KPI stands for *key performance indicators*.

As academics and consultants explain this jargon, key result areas are the primary components or parts of the job in which a person is expected to deliver results. Key performance indicators represent the measures that will be used to determine how well the individual has performed. In other words, KRAs tell where the individual is supposed to concentrate her attention; KPIs tell how her performance in the specified areas should be measured.

Probably few parts of the performance appraisal process create more misunderstanding and bewilderment than do the notion of KRAs and KPIs. The reason is that so much of the material written about KPIs and KRAs is both confusing and contradictory. One article says that KRAs should never contain a verb. "Patient care," according to this source, is a KRA, but if the verb *provide* is added to turn the statement into "Provide patient care," then the rules for writing KRAs have been violated. Another authority argues that the measures used in KPIs can only be quantitative and must be limited exclusively to those things that can be expressed in numbers. Both of these statements are not only false, but they also serve to make what should be a straightforward procedure incomprehensible to ordinary organization members and their managers. Let's make it simple.

Turning KRAs into Big Rocks

A few years ago I was asked by one of America's most clandestine intelligence agencies to help them design a new performance appraisal system. This agency, charged with intercepting and deciphering the messages that America's enemies were sending in order to intercept any threats and safeguard our security, had been under congressional pressure to develop an effective performance appraisal system. A group of in-house HR practitioners had developed a prototype and arranged for a pilot test of the new form and performance appraisal system with a group of agency managers.

The planned day-long pilot session broke up less than an hour after it had started, the developers told me later, when one of the managers interrupted their explanation of the new appraisal procedures by exclaiming, "Wait a minute! This won't work! All the people who work for me are mathematicians. They may spend all day just staring out the window. And yet they're doing their jobs. How do I evaluate their performance?"

When the team and I started working together after the failure of the initial prototype to help managers assess performance, I suggested that we begin with the issue that created the stumbling block in the rollout session: How do you evaluate the performance of a mathematician, who may spend a good deal of time staring out the window, but is still "doing his job"?

I suggested that they imagine themselves talking with one of the agency's mathematicians and asking, "What are the big rocks in your job?" "Big rocks," I explained, was an informal, understandable, and quite helpful phrase to get people to center on the most important elements of their job.

What Are "Big Rocks"?

Any job involves dozens, even hundreds, of different tasks and activities. But all of these tasks and activities are done to meet a small number of vital responsibilities. These are the key job responsibilities of the job. Thinking of them as "big rocks" makes it easy for people to sort through all the busyness and chores and duties they get involved in and to look at the bigger picture. It helps them identify the small number of unique responsibilities that must be performed successfully if the job is to be considered to be done well. The big rocks are the most important responsibilities of a job—the responsibilities that are the reason for engaging in all the activities and tasks.

It turns out, I told the team, that a job may seem to be so complex that it's virtually impossible for someone who hasn't had years of highly specialized training to perform it at all, let alone do it well. A mathematician, for example. But while doing all the tasks and activities of a mathematician may be impossible for someone without specialized training, getting a handle on the purpose or reason for all this activity is usually fairly easy.

So give the mathematician thirty seconds of explanation and then ask, "What are the big rocks in your job?"

With little hesitation or coaching, the mathematician will respond, "I create numerical algorithms."

Without needing to understand what a numerical algorithm is, you simply write down, "Create numerical algorithms." You then ask, "Is that it? Is that the only big rock? Are there any other major responsibilities in your job?"

"Of course," the mathematician replies. "I figure out ways to resolve those algorithms. And I develop software. And I make sure that we maintain good relationships with the universities and think tanks that we work with."

"Anything else?" you ask.

"No, that's about it," the mathematician replies.

At that point, the key job responsibilities of the mathematician's job have been identified:

Create numerical algorithms

Analyze and resolve numerical algorithms

Write software

Maintain relationships with universities and think tanks

And as a consequence, the key result areas—the KRAs—have been identified. Identifying KRAs is precisely that simple. Thinking about big rocks removes the mystery that seems to surround the notion of KRAs.[1]

Notice a few things about the big rocks the mathematician identified in his job. First, they are very simply stated. Essentially, each is just a verb (*write, create, maintain*) coupled with a noun (*software, numerical algorithms, relationships*). There's no indication in the big rock statement of how often the person engages in this activity, what its components are, how the quality of performance will be measured, or how important it is to the individual's overall success. It is a simple statement in verb/noun form of each of the key responsibilities of someone with the job of mathematician.

Notice also that there aren't very many big rocks. That's true in the mathematician's job, and it's true in the jobs of almost anyone who works in an organization, regardless of the individual's level in the hierarchy or the apparent complexity of the position. All of us do dozens of chores and hundreds of tasks daily and weekly, but we do them in order to accomplish a small number of key job responsibilities.

Another element of big rocks is that each is independent of the others. There isn't any overlap. Big rocks are stand-alone features of the job; they're not the same things expressed in different ways.

Finally, the big rocks themselves give us no information on the quality of performance or how that quality will be measured. Big rock statements don't say "Write efficient software" or "Maintain harmonious and productive relationships." As important as quality and measurement are, they will be addressed later.

Identifying the big rocks of any job is actually fairly uncomplicated and straightforward, most easily accomplished simply by giving the person a quick overview of the process, providing a list of examples of the key job responsibilities for a couple of other jobs, and asking her to generate the same list for her own position.

For a salesman, the big rocks list might include the following items:

Acquire new business

Retain existing customers

Sell product

Manage territory

Generate leads

File reports

Again, notice that the big rocks list doesn't specify how much new business the salesman is expected to generate, the volume of sales, the quality of leads, or anything other than a simple verb/noun statement of the key job responsibilities.

For a school bus driver, the big rocks might include:

Drive bus

Greet students and parents

Ensure bus maintenance

Control student behavior

For other jobs, an individual's big rocks list might include items like the following:

Enter data	Resolve complaints
Negotiate contracts	Create architectural drawings
Conduct hearings	Lead team
Screen applicants	Coordinate services
Diagnose equipment problems	Evaluate performance
Balance accounts	Update software
Schedule appointments	Identify potential acquisitions
Sanitize facilities	Keep users informed

Notice that this big rocks list includes responsibilities that cover a wide range of jobs in the organizational hierarchy. One of the CEO's big rocks might be to "identify potential acquisitions"; it's the janitor's job to "sanitize facilities."

There are several advantages to preparing the big rocks list jointly with the individual who's doing the job. First, for you as the manager it provides a good test of whether the individual's view of what's really important in her job squares with yours. If there are discrepancies, it's much better to find out about them at the start of the year instead of at performance appraisal time and have the person react to a low rating by arguing that she was unaware she was responsible for the low-rated area of the job.

Another advantage is that it's easy for people to spend their time in those parts of the job where they excel; those parts of the job that—regardless of importance—they most enjoy or find most valuable. Identifying the job's big rocks helps redirect their attention toward what's really important.

There are other sources of information to help you identify the big rocks in a job besides your own analysis, the information in the job description, and the insights of the person who's actually doing the job. Talking to peers who supervise similar positions may be helpful. And looking at the way that those who are considered top performers spend their time may shed light on what's genuinely important.

How Do We Measure Successful Performance?

By identifying the big rocks or key job responsibilities, we have identified the KRAs—the key result areas. *KRAs, big rocks,* and *key job responsibilities* are simply different terms for the same thing.

The other task involved in identifying a person's key job responsibilities is determining how each one of these big rocks or KRAs will be measured. What will the individual need to do to be considered as performing successfully? What are the key performance indicators—the KPIs of this job?

To determine appropriate measures for each big rock in a job, start by asking questions:

- What does excellence look like?

- What are top performers doing when carrying out this key responsibility?

- How will we know when an employee has mastered a key job responsibility? What will indicate that the person is truly performing at a superior level?

- What will it look like when an employee is fully successful in carrying out this key job responsibility?

- How will you—or anyone else—know that success in this key job responsibility has been achieved?

- What will you see when this part of the job is done particularly well?

- What's a specific example of this part of the job done particularly well?[2]

As you consider these questions, recognize that there are only four measures of output: quality, quantity, cost, and timeliness. For each of the big rocks that you've identified, look for indicators that shed light on how well the individual performed (quality), the amount of work the person did (quantity), the degree to which the person adhered to the budget or was cost-conscious in going about the job (cost), and the extent to which schedules and deadlines were met (timeliness).

For some of these measures, quantitative measures will be easy to determine, particularly when our concern involves quantity, cost, or timeliness: How many units did the salesman sell? Did Jane complete her project within the budget or did she exceed it, and by how much? Was Wally's assignment completed by the deadline, ahead of schedule, or late?

For assessing the quality of someone's performance, quantitative measures may not be available. For our mathematician, it may be easy to identify the number of software programs written, but there may not be a numerical, quantitative measure that sheds much light on the quality of the software she produced. Software developers admire someone who can write "elegant code." But where's the quantitative measure of elegance?

In chapter 6 we'll focus directly on how to measure and evaluate performance. For the purpose of identifying how each of the big rocks, or KRAs, of a job will be measured, it's enough to point out that two kinds of measures can be used: *quantitative* and *descriptive*. If your concern involves the quantity of work done, or the cost incurred, or the timeliness of the individual's performance, it will be easy to find workable quantitative measures. For assessing the quality of performance, however, there may not be good quantitative measures that accurately indicate exactly how well the person performed. In this case you can describe the quality of performance using examples.

For each key job responsibility or big rock, identify a half dozen measures that will give you a good indication about the extent to which the job was performed at a fully successful level. To illustrate, table 3-1 gives a list of the big rocks, the measures, and the examples of fully successful performance by a registered nurse created by consultant Jack Zigon.

TABLE 3-1

Key job responsibilities and measures for a registered nurse

"Big rocks"	Measures/examples of fully successful performance
Provide patient care	No patient falls. Medication dosages are proper; alert to responses to medication based on patient condition and age. No medication errors during the course of year. Rapid patient admission and assessment. No transmission of pathogens. Patient care follows the prescribed plan of care.
Assess patients	Assessment for signs and symptoms of abuse or neglect are performed and documented; reporting procedures are followed. Age-specific nutritional assessment is performed and documented and referrals made as necessary. Documentation of assessment complies with time stated in the policies. Cultural and religious beliefs are assessed and considered in plan and delivery of care. Physician, manager, or hospital resource person are satisfied that: • All patients are accurately and thoroughly assessed as per policy. • Appropriate actions are taken upon changes in patient status. • Changes are identified and assessed before a crisis occurs.
Educate patients and families	Patient and family are aware of patient diagnosis, medications, and treatments they must administer. RN receives unsolicited compliments from patient or family. Provisions are made for those who do not speak or read English.

(continued)

TABLE 3-1 (CONTINUED)

Key job responsibilities and measures for a registered nurse

"Big rocks"	Measures/examples of fully successful performance
Coordinate services	Checks emails each shift. Utilized by other departments or staff as a resource. Communication with other care providers is timely, accurate, and complete.
Assure patient and physician satisfaction	No justified complaints from patients or family. When asked, patients and family say: • The nurse introduced herself, explained all tests and procedures, and kept me informed about what was going on. • The nurse understands how I feel. • I received my pain medication quickly. • The nurse respected my privacy and confidentiality. No justified physician complaints. When asked, physicians say that the nurse: • Called me only when appropriate. • Had all information I needed when asked.

Source: Jack Zigon, *Sample Employee Performance Measures,* rev. ed. (Wallingford, PA: Zigon Performance Group, 1996).

A few things in the list of key job responsibilities of the registered nurse's job are worth highlighting. First, note that while some of the measures are quantitative ("No patient falls"), others can't be measured using numbers; but the quality of performance can certainly be described using examples ("Cultural and religious beliefs are assessed and considered in plan and delivery of care").

Even some of the quantitative measures incorporate an element of managerial judgment. Notice that one of the measures provided for "Assure patient and physician satisfaction" is "No justified complaints from patients or family." While it may be easy to count the number of complaints received from patients and their families, a wiser measure is to count only the number of justified complaints, and ignore those complaints that resulted from the nurse's doing her job exactly as it should be done, even though that action resulted in a baseless patient complaint. A complaint that the nurse served food that was bland and tasteless shouldn't be counted in evaluating the nurse's performance.

The Benefit of Big Rocks and Key Measures of Successful Performance

Identifying an individual's key job responsibilities or big rocks (the KRAs of the job) and the measures or examples of fully successful performance (the KPIs of the job) provides several benefits—particularly if you do this together with the individual whose job is being analyzed. Most important, it clarifies exactly what the most significant responsibilities of the job are, so the individual is less likely to waste time working on low-payoff activities. It provides much clearer direction than a job description can since it focuses on the specific job done by a specific individual and not the generic requirements that apply to anyone with that job title.

When there are several individuals who perform exactly the same job (a group of nurses, customer service representatives, or IT techs, for example), doing the assessment of big rocks and key performance measures as a group can not only be a powerful team-building experience, it can also clarify for the entire group exactly what the manager's or the company's expectations are for the people who fill that role. Even better, by working as a group, people can identify those responsibilities that have been assigned to specific individuals and aren't shared universally by everyone else on the team.

Identifying a set of measures and examples of fully successful performance will answer the question asked by every organization member: What do you expect of me? Clarifying what "fully successful" performance looks like lets people know the level at which they will need to perform in order to be seen as meeting expectations.

Finally, identifying key job responsibilities and providing examples of fully successful performance greatly reduce the chances that there will be surprises in the performance appraisal discussion. The individual may not agree with the supervisor's assessment, but he won't be able to argue that he didn't know what he was expected to do or how his performance would be evaluated.

Principles to Remember

DO

✓ Think about the key responsibility areas (KRAs) of a job as "big rocks."

✓ Spell out the big rocks of a job in simple verb/noun format.

✓ Use descriptive measures and examples, not numbers, to measure the quality of an individual's performance.

DON'T

✓ Be confused by the terms *KRAs*, *key job responsibilities*, and *big rocks*—they're just different names for the same thing.

✓ Focus excessively on finding numeric, quantitative performance measures.

✓ Try to describe performance at an ideal or Exceeds Expectations level—just be clear about what Fully Successful looks like.

Chapter **4**

Identifying and Using Competencies

In chapter 1 I explained that job performance is made up of two separate components: what the person accomplishes and how the person goes about achieving those results. Goal setting and identifying the key responsibilities of the job—the *results* dimension of performance—were the subjects of chapters 2 and 3. In this chapter we turn to the other half of performance—the behaviors or competencies that generate those results.

Competencies describe the knowledge, skills, behaviors, attributes, abilities, and attitudes that are essential to achieving the results expected. A competency is a significant talent, skill, or proficiency that helps an individual generate superior performance. The reason for identifying competencies is to let everyone know that in this company (or department or work unit), there are a small number of genuinely important behaviors that the leader will be paying close attention to and be holding every member of the team accountable for displaying in their day-to-day performance.

It's useful to recognize that there are three kinds of competencies: core competencies, job-family competencies, and job-specific competencies.

Core (or *cultural* or *organizational*) *competencies* are the competencies that everyone who works for the organization is expected to demonstrate, regardless of the individual's job or position in the hierarchy. A company might include such items as communication skills, interpersonal skills, and continuous improvement among its core competencies. No matter what a person's specific job duties or place in the hierarchy, it's reasonable to expect every member of the team to communicate well, to get along with others, and to look for ways in which the job can be done better.

Job-family competencies are those that for a particular type or classification of job—sales, for example, or operations, administrative functions, or customer service—are vital to successful performance. For a person who works in the *operations* family of jobs (blue collar, hourly, trades employees), the competencies expected might include dependability, follow-up, protection of assets, and safety. For individuals in the *supervisory/managerial* job family, the list of competencies might include team leadership, motivating subordinates and others, and developing and retaining talent. Employees in the *administrative* job family might have time management, planning and organizing, and professional presence/business demeanor on their competency list.

Finally, *job-specific competencies* represent the explicit skills and abilities that are required to perform a particular job at a successful level. For a trench digger, these competencies might be backhoe operation, the ability to read construction drawings, and the knowledge of construction site safety requirements. For an operations manager, the competencies required might include negotiating skills, blueprint reading, and conflict-resolution skills.

Core Competencies

For the most part, the identification of core or organization-wide competencies is beyond the scope of individual managers. Occasionally a manager is asked to serve on a task force charged with identifying a set of core competencies that the senior executive team might consider as the competencies that every organization member will be expected to demonstrate. Typically, however, those core competencies are determined by the owner, managing partner, or senior executive team of an organization.

For the individual leader, what is important about core competencies is figuring out how the people he or she supervises will be expected to demonstrate these competencies, and how the manager plans to assess the quality of their performance on each. A well-drafted competency statement will contain an easy-to-understand description of exactly what individuals are expected to do to demonstrate excellence in each of the company's core or organization-wide competencies.

If a simple description of each competency does not exist, the manager will have to do the job herself. She'll need to look at her operation and determine how she expects people to demonstrate the company's competencies in their day-to-day performance and how she will assess each person's performance in each competency area at the end of the year.

Get your team involved. An effective way to approach this task is to circulate the list of organizational competencies to the members of the team and ask them for their insights and suggestions on how to make the core competency list come alive in their department. Their responses will not only generate some specific ideas about how team members can demonstrate mastery of the company's core competencies in their approach to their work and the department's day-to-day activities, they will also guarantee that everyone in the department will be familiar with the corporate expectations and unsurprised when their performance is evaluated against each of the core competencies at year-end. Even better, ask them to come up with nonexamples as well as examples. The nonexamples may illustrate what is expected (and not expected) in every competency area much more clearly than the examples themselves can.

Job-Family and Job-Specific Competencies

If competencies for specific jobs and job families have already been determined and publicized in the organization, then the responsibility of the manager is the same as it is with the core competencies: to figure out how each competency shows up in department members' jobs and to plan for how the competencies will be assessed on the performance appraisal. If job competencies haven't been identified, there's a high payoff in developing a list of the most important behaviors the leader expects people in his or her department to demonstrate.

Since many managers supervise people with two significantly different types of jobs—supervisors and individual contributors—it may be productive to consider developing separate lists to emphasize the different nature of these two jobs. But there's no reason why competencies can't overlap and appear on both lists. For example, "problem solving" might appear on the competency list for both supervisory and individual contributor positions. There's probably no need for the manager to refine the list any further than separating it into "supervisory competencies" and "individual contributor competencies." It's rarely necessary to create separate lists for different job families, even though some of the employees may be in the professional/technical job family, others in the administrative job family, and some in the operations job family. The goal is to make things simple, not complex.

Success depends on keeping the list short, straightforward, and easy to understand. You're not trying to take over a piece of HR's job here. Your goal is to let people know what behaviors you consider important and will hold them responsible for. You will hold them accountable for demonstrating these behaviors in their annual performance appraisal, where performance (or nonperformance) will directly impact their ratings, salaries, and promotional opportunities. And you'll hold them accountable in the ongoing coaching sessions you conduct whenever a person performs in a way that attracts your notice, either positively or negatively.

How to Identify Competencies

Begin by identifying a small number—three to five is ideal, certainly no more than seven or eight—of the behaviors, skills, or attributes that you feel are genuinely important in getting the job done the way you want it to be done. These can be competencies that group members are currently deficient in and need to improve, or ones that are currently being demonstrated at an acceptable level and whose importance you want to reinforce. You can decide on these by yourself, or you can get the input of your team members.

Why limit the list to so few? The smaller the number, the more important each one is. If people are faced with a list of a dozen or more competencies that you want them to demonstrate, the individual importance of each item becomes trivial and the entire list will be quickly forgotten.

Where do you find lists of competencies that should be considered in identifying the core competencies that will apply to everyone? Many companies have developed a competency model, and the set of competencies appropriate for different jobs and job families may already have been provided. If your company hasn't created a list of competencies, go online; they're easy to find with a quick Internet search. One of the best lists was developed by New York State and is available for public use on the state's Web site.[1] *Workforce* magazine's Web site provides a list of thirty-one competencies, including definitions and observable behaviors, that can help indicate the degree to which a person demonstrates the competency.[2]

The truth is, the source of the list makes little difference. The important thing is to select a small number of important behaviors that you feel will make a significant difference in the quality of the performance of the people in your work group, however large or small that group may be.

How to Describe Performance Excellence

The first step is simply to generate the list of competencies, with smaller-is-better governing the number of competencies you choose. Once you've developed the list, your next step is to describe for each one what excellent performance looks like.

If the competency list you used already has behavioral descriptions of excellent performance, you can edit them so they apply directly to the type of work done by the people in your group. If behavioral descriptions aren't available, or if they are written in competency jargon and HR-speak to the extent that they don't give people solid direction on exactly what they should do, simply write your own descriptions of what good performance for each of the competencies would look like.

It's not hard. Begin by asking a couple of questions:

- For this competency, what does excellent performance look like?

- In this area, what would someone who's a true role model be likely to do that you wouldn't expect an average performer to do?

- What would be a specific example that illustrates mastery of this skill, knowledge, or attitude?

- What would make you sit up and say, "There! That's what I'm looking for!"

Remember that you're not trying to *define* what the competency means. Providing a dictionary definition is not the goal. Your goal is to provide your people with guidelines for excellence, explaining in everyday language what they need to do in order to be considered an outstanding performer in this area.

Here are some examples of effective competency descriptions. The first two are for competencies that might be considered universal—appropriate for everyone in a company. The second two describe performance in a specialized area, competencies that might apply to only a tiny number of employees in an organization but that would be critical to overall success in their jobs.

Attendance/Punctuality/Dependability: Comes to work on time every day. Is fully prepared and ready to work at beginning of work schedule and continues until work day is done. Makes appropriate arrangements when adverse weather or other problems might delay on-time arrival. Conforms to work hours and schedule. Lets supervisor and others know immediately when unexpected problems cause absence, lateness, or the need to leave early.

Job Knowledge/Technical Skills: Is an expert in doing his or her job. Seen as a resource by others. Has a great deal of relevant experience. Makes good suggestions about ways to improve. Can explain the mission of both his or her own work unit, other units, and how they work together to meet organizational objectives. Makes active efforts to stay up-to-date. Requires minimal supervision.

Relationship Building: Builds and maintains a network of contacts useful in achieving work-related goals. Extends and accepts invitations from others to build effective working relationships. Skilled in building rapport with a wide variety of individuals. Understands the balance between taking time to build rapport and getting the work done. Sensitive to what people around him or her are feeling. Promotes the contributions and accomplishments of customers or clients to others. Enthusiastic about others' ideas.

Strategic Thinking: Understands and can explain the organization's mission and its plan for achieving it. Develops strategies to achieve department and organizational goals. Clearly understands market, customers, competition, and technology. Demonstrates a track record of significant and successful innovation. Knows organization's strengths, weaknesses, opportunities, and threats. Moves beyond "cheaper/faster/better" to seek truly transformational change. Carefully considers and successfully implements ideas that seem nontraditional or radical. Quickly adapts strategy to respond to changing conditions. Able to develop persuasive and compelling long-term (three- to five-year) plans.

Notice that each of the competency descriptions contains several different behaviors. "Attendance/punctuality/dependability," for example, involves more than just showing up every day on time. A person who's a role model in this area would do more than that. He would make advance preparations when a forecast of bad weather or anticipated heavy traffic might make getting to work more difficult than usual. He would let his boss and other team members know immediately when some problem arose that might cause lateness or absence at some future date.

Another technique that works well is to describe both helpful and hurtful behaviors for each competency. It's as important to tell people what not to do in each competency area as it is to let them know what stellar performance looks like.

Putting the Competency List to Work

The final step is to publicize the competency list with the descriptions of expert-level behaviors. People really do want to know what's expected of them.

Once the competency list has been developed and explained, it becomes part of the performance requirements of every person on the team—including you. Followers have expectations of their leaders just as the leaders do of the team members. Letting people know that you won't wait until performance appraisal time to inform them of how they're doing in meeting the expectations spelled out in the competency document, and that you want to hear from them if there's a leadership competency you need to brush up on, makes everyone accountable for excellence in performance.

Principles to Remember

DO

✓ Recognize that *competencies* is just the fancy term for the behavioral part of job performance.

✓ Let people know which behaviors and competencies are the most important to you.

✓ Keep the list of competencies short.

DON'T

✓ Try to identify all the important competencies by your-self—get your team involved.

✓ Be concerned if the same competency shows up for different jobs.

✓ Write a dictionary definition for each competency—just provide examples of what effective performance looks like.

Chapter **5**

Providing Day-to-Day Coaching

In the first few chapters I talked about the elements of performance appraisal that take place at the beginning of every appraisal cycle. At that time, you need to spend about an hour with each of the people on your team setting goals, reviewing their key job responsibilities (including any changes to those responsibilities since they were reviewed the year before), and discussing the competencies or behaviors that you expect your employees to demonstrate.

Once goals, responsibilities, and competencies are clear, people can do their jobs with the peace of mind that comes from having clear direction. Your primary performance appraisal responsibility between the end of the performance planning session and the end-of-year performance appraisal is to provide coaching for your team members to help them increase the quality of their performance.

Frequent coaching during the year is vital. It lowers the fear factor people may experience during the annual appraisal discussion if that's the only time the boss talks about performance. Goals and directions change more rapidly than a once-a-year appraisal can accommodate, and coaching can redirect effort toward revised priorities. People are more likely to ask for help if guidance is offered in informal reviews. Particularly valuable is coaching that is focused on reinforcing effective performance. Too often managers' coaching time is spent only on problem solving.

People notice poor-quality and nonexistent coaching. In a survey of its member companies, some of America's largest and best managed firms, the Corporate Leadership Council reported that only 34 percent of employees felt that the informal feedback they received was fair and accurate, and more than two-thirds disagreed with the statement, "The informal feedback I receive helps me do my job better."[1]

When to Coach

Knowing when to step in to coach someone on the team is one of the real challenges managers face. Coaching can easily fall into the realm of good intentions, something that happens only "one of these days" unless we schedule it. The key is to conduct routine coaching sessions in addition to those that arise because of a specific problem or issue—to make coaching both calendar- and event-driven.

Calendar-Driven Coaching Sessions

In the performance planning session at the start of the year, close the meeting by setting a date for a status update. Three months is a reasonable time frame. Writing a specific date on each person's calendar increases the probability that the meeting will happen. The date may later have to be moved because of schedule conflicts. But it's like a routine dentist appointment—you may have to reschedule, but you're not going to stop going to the dentist. After that first session, set a date for the next follow-up.

In conducting a calendar-driven coaching session, start by asking, "What major events have taken place since the last time we got together?" Then spend the next forty-five minutes or so reviewing the major activities that occurred, successes, problems, and lessons learned.

Midyear reviews. Many companies request or require managers to hold a midyear review meeting with each person on the team. It's a good idea to use the performance appraisal form to structure the agenda for the meeting, highlighting areas of particular success and areas where performance needs to be improved. But don't send the midyear appraisal form to the individual's official personnel file, unless that's mandated. By using the form but keeping it just between yourself and the employee, it's easier to underscore serious performance deficiencies while at the same time allowing the opportunity for correction before a permanent "black mark" appears on the official year-end appraisal. Keep the completed midyear review form with other departmental personnel information, and use it as one of your data sources when the time comes for completing the final performance appraisal.

Another major benefit of conducting a planned midyear review is that it allows for updating goals that have been achieved or abandoned and for adding new projects that have been undertaken. It's also a good time to adjust the list of key job responsibilities if a significant amount of the individual's work time is being spent in areas not included in the original list.

Event-Driven Reviews

Any of these events should trigger a leader-initiated coaching session:

- After the completion of a major project, regardless of the outcome. Coaching is particularly valuable—and appreciated—when it follows a significant success.

- When one of your employees is experiencing difficulties in getting a job done.

- When an individual is expressing frustration or dissatisfaction with the job.

- When an individual's mood or temperament on the job varies from the norm for that person, and the mood swing or temperament change lasts more than a couple of days.

What Is Coaching?

Coaching involves learning from experience. Experience may be a good teacher, but unless we reflect on that experience it won't be a very effective one. It will just be an event. What the manager needs to do through coaching is put the experience in context.

Before employees can benefit from coaching, however, they must have the appropriate training and skills. Training comes first, coaching comes second. Employees must also know what's expected of them and how their performance will be measured. Employee coaching is designed to help people overcome performance barriers. If the people who work for you don't know what performance is expected of them, they won't know how to get there.

In more specific terms, coaching involves the following functions:[2]

- Giving *advice* to help employees improve their performance. The manager typically brings more experience to the situation that the employee needs help with. Giving advice doesn't mean telling the person how to do the job, but offering suggestions based on your experience.

- Providing employees with *guidance* so that they can develop their skills and knowledge appropriately. Coaching involves providing help with both the knowledge and the skills needed to do the job, and information about how the employee can acquire these skills and knowledge.

- Providing employees *support* (but being there only when your presence is needed). Coaching involves being available when the individual needs help, but not monitoring and controlling the employee's every move. The responsibility for performance, and improving that performance to meet the requirements of the job, is the employee's.

- Giving employees *confidence* that will enable them to enhance their performance continuously and increase their ability to manage their own performance. Coaching involves giving positive feedback that allows people to feel confident about what they're doing and how they're doing it, as well as letting them know about areas where they need to improve.

- Helping employees gain greater *competence* by guiding them toward acquiring more knowledge and sharpening their skills so that they are better prepared for more complex tasks and higher-level positions.

What Coaching Isn't

Coaching isn't training. Coaching happens after training is completed. Training's job is to make people competent; coaching's job is to make them masters.

Coaching isn't telling people how to do their jobs or explaining precisely the way you want something done. That's called micromanaging.

Coaching isn't counseling. Coaching focuses on work issues; counseling focuses on personal issues. But a coaching session can inadvertently turn into a counseling session if the employee starts talking about a non-work-related issue that impacts job performance—such as financial troubles, family relationships, health problems, or drug or alcohol issues. When this happens, the manager needs to immediately redirect the discussion: "Jim, we're getting into an area that, while it is important, is none of my business. I'm not qualified to give you any help or suggestions."

If your company has an employee assistance program (EAP), make the employee aware of it, without directly telling the person that he or she needs to contact the EAP provider (it's the employee's responsibility to make the decision to get help and to make the contact). If your company doesn't have an EAP, say something like this: "Les, I've got a responsibility to make sure that everyone is performing at full capacity while they're on the job, and it sounds like you've got a situation off the job that's getting in the way. I probably can't be helpful to you with that. What do you think you might do to get this situation resolved?"

Then listen. If the response seems at all reasonable, say, "I hope that works for you. In the meantime, let's focus on what you need to do to meet all your job responsibilities, so concerns about your job won't distract from your being able to get this other situation taken care of." Again, coaching isn't counseling. As a manager you're unqualified to offer counseling. Don't get in over your head.

Mandatory Coaching Situations

We need to let people make their own mistakes so they can learn from them. We can train and advise them, which will help some of the time, but actual experience is often the best teacher. The wise manager, therefore, will generally hang back and resist the impulse to jump in every time an employee encounters difficulty. A good manager, however, will always monitor what her employees are doing and will directly intervene to coach an employee whenever the following circumstances occur:

- Their current behavior poses a threat to themselves or someone else. When an employee is doing something that could cause harm to themselves or someone else, you have to step in. This is one instance where you can't let someone learn from their mistakes. You need to provide coaching. If possible, rather than telling the person the solution, suggest a couple of alternatives and let the individual figure out which is best. Make sure that the employee understands why the behavior he or she is planning is inappropriate.

- There are ethical or legal ramifications of their actions. You can't allow employees to do things that are illegal or unethical, regardless of whether they are acting with intent or out of ignorance. As with dangerous behaviors, provide alternatives, let them decide, and explain why the planned behavior is a poor choice.

- They are hurting their team membership. You need your employees to work together as a team. If one member is doing something that will cause the others to exclude him from the team, you have to step in. If an employee always takes credit for the team's work, you need to tell her to stop. If an employee in a cubicle often yells into the phone and disturbs those around him, you have to step in and insist on change.

- They are repeating failed behaviors. When someone has repeatedly tried to solve a problem and his solution still isn't working, you need to get involved. Often we try something and it fails. We may try it again to make sure we did it the way we intended. It still fails. If a person, however, keeps trying after a second failure, he isn't learning. The manager needs to step in and provide coaching.

- The financial impact on the company is severe. Almost any mistake is going to cost the company money, either directly or in lost time or other ways. You can't step in every time an employee might make a mistake just to save money—consider it an investment in the employee's learning and development. However, if the planned action will have a significant negative financial effect, you have to get involved. You have a responsibility to the company to protect its fiscal assets that's just as great as your responsibility to develop its human assets. Provide the employee with alternative behaviors, let her figure out the appropriate choice, and explain why you had to step in.[3]

- Their current performance varies significantly from what past performance appraisals have described. It may well be that all the individual's past reviews have (inaccurately) described her as a star performer. In this case, when you talk with the individual, it's appropriate to say something like, "Elaine, I noticed that all of your past performance appraisals have described you as an excellent performer. But I haven't seen that level of performance in this job. Let me tell you about what I've observed . . . " Past performance appraisals can be a useful source of data and insights whenever you initiate a coaching session based on a concern about the individual's performance. Check the person's past reviews to see whether previous supervisors have commented on the same concern you find the need to address now. If that's the case, make reference to those earlier performance appraisals in discussing the issue with the individual.

A Complete Coaching Session Example

Here's an example of a successful coaching session. In this example, you'll meet Tom and Anne. Anne is a fairly new employee who was highly recruited and has a hard-to-find skill set. Tom, Anne's boss, worked hard to recruit her and feels that she has a lot of potential. Tom truly wants Anne to be successful, but he's aware that she's struggling. They are together for Anne's midyear review.

As you read the exchange between Tom and Anne, pay attention to what he's doing as he coaches her. While the script may seem long on paper, the actual conversation between the two probably takes less than five minutes.

Tom: It's been about six months since we had the review and talked about what you'll be doing in the upcoming year. I know we've talked briefly about how you've been coming along, but now that we're about halfway through the year I wanted to spend some time really talking about how things are going for you. Tell me—how are things going?

Anne: They're fine. The quality project is coming along well. And it should, with the hours I've put in on it.

Tom: Bring me up to date.

Anne: Well, not a lot to tell. We ran into a problem with the first milestone when we didn't get the support we were counting on from Simpson, but since then things have been pretty good.

Tom: What happened?

Anne: He quit, remember? We knew he was going to be leaving, but I didn't anticipate how much his not being here would slow us down.

Tom: We missed two milestones.

Anne: Well, yeah. One thing spiraled into another. You know how it is. But I think I've gotten it back on track now.

Tom: I'm concerned, Anne. It's an important project, and we've missed two key dates. That doesn't sound like "coming along well."

Anne: I think things are going to be OK. I don't think you have to be concerned.

Tom: Well, perhaps you're right. But two missed milestones is serious. I'm concerned that you knew Simpson was going to be leaving but waited until he was gone to look for someone to fill in for him. And on the second one, I didn't know that you weren't going to make the deadline until a day before.

Anne: I was hoping that we'd make it. I didn't bring it to your attention because I really didn't think we were going to miss. I let you know as soon as I realized that it just wasn't going to happen, no matter how much time I put in. And I did put in time, lots of it. Do you know how much time I put in?

Tom: No, I don't. But putting in time isn't the problem. Actually, maybe it *is* the problem. You're putting in time when you should be managing a project. You didn't plan for the impact of Simpson's departure until he'd actually left, and then you tried to make up for it by putting in lots of your own time. And you didn't let me know until just before it happened that the last deadline was going to be missed. (*Pause.*) I'm worried, Anne. Should I be?

Anne: What are you saying, Tom? What's the real message? Am I in trouble?

Tom: No, not "in trouble," but I'm concerned. I put you in charge of the quality project because I thought you were ready for taking on something bigger. But it doesn't seem to be working out.

Anne: Look, I am doing my best. Simpson was no help to me once he told us he was leaving. The people on my team, I don't know, it's like they think the assignments that I give them aren't as important as the things they do for other people. So they leave my stuff till the last minute. And I'm not their boss . . . I can't say "I'm gonna fire you unless you get this done by Tuesday." I don't feel like I'm getting their respect as project leader.

Tom: What do you mean?

Anne: They've all got a couple of projects they're working on. But nobody sees this quality project as the most important one they've got. I do, but I'm the only one. I think they work on my project only when their other stuff is done.

Tom: Why do you think that is?

Anne: I don't know. Maybe I don't crack the whip hard enough. But I'm not their boss, so I can't say, "Do it or else!" So I guess I find that it's easier, when schedules start slipping, to just get in there and do things myself.

Tom: And what's the result of doing that?

Anne: Well, one result is that I'm overwhelmed with my current workload.

Tom: You're overwhelmed, and the results on the quality project—at least at this point—aren't satisfactory. (*Anne looks at him, startled.*) The results you've produced on the quality project so far—not making plans for

Simpson's departure, missing two deadlines, not letting me know about problems until the last minute, as well as not managing to get the support of the people on your team . . . You and I both know that this isn't satisfactory.

Anne: Tom, my work has never been unsatisfactory.

Tom: That's true. And it's also true that you've never had a challenge like this before. You may have always relied completely on yourself in the past, and that seems to have worked for you. Now I am looking to you to be successful as a leader of a very important project that has a big impact on our business.

Anne: Yeah, I know. Are you going to hand my quality project off to somebody else?

Tom: No. It's you. And I haven't changed my mind that you can do this. But not the way you've been doing it so far.

Anne: So what do I do?

Tom: Well, a couple things are obvious, and you've probably already noticed them yourself. When you find out about something that's going to cause delays in your schedule, like Simpson's departure, get to work on backup plans so that you don't end up doing everything yourself. And don't let me get caught by surprise when a deadline's going to be missed or something else happens. But the big thing is getting people on your team to see you as a leader, whether or not you're their boss.

Anne: Yeah, well, OK. But I don't know exactly what I should do. Should I go to a training program or something on project management?

Tom: Well, maybe, if the right program comes along. But we can't wait for a training program. This is something that we need to work on right now. But I believe you already have the talent and skills to make this project successful.

Anne: Yes . . .

Tom: Look, you're an engineer. A good one. You know how to figure things out. Let's try to figure this out. You've got to get the people on the team working together, and giving you what you need, without being able to say, "Do it because I said so." So how can you do it?

Anne: I don't know. Other people seem to be able to do this. But it's something new to me.

Tom: OK. Let's think about the people you've known who have been really good team leaders. What did they do that you're not doing?

Anne: Oh. I'm not sure. I hadn't thought about it like that. Maybe I can pay attention to what you do in working with us and, I don't know, maybe make up a list or something.

Tom: Well, perhaps. But I may not be the best person to work with you on this. (*Pause.*) Look, I'm here to help. I want you to be successful and I'm sure that you can. And I'm happy to look over anything you want me to. But the more I do to help you be successful, the more it's me that's succeeding and not you. I'd suggest that you think about other people who are facing the same kind of situation you are. You've worked on lots of teams; you know who's able to get everybody pulling together.

Anne: Yeah, Gwen Morrissey. Everybody respects her. And she gets great results.

Tom: So why don't you think about what she does and come up with some ideas. See what she does and how you might do the same kinds of things, but in your own way. Talk your ideas over with her. I'll be happy to give you my own feedback, too, but I really expect you to take ownership of the project.

Anne: So where do we go from here?

Tom: Well, I've got some other things we should go over, but we've covered the one that was really on my mind. Project management's tough, and it's particularly tough when everybody on the project team is getting pulled in a bunch of different directions. I know you can handle it. But you need to get right to work...

Analyzing Tom's Coaching Session with Anne

The dialogue between Tom and Anne illustrates several key coaching points:

Listening: Throughout the conversation Tom listened closely to what Anne was saying. He was able several times to reflect accurately what she had said to him.

Using a straightforward approach: Tom was frank—almost blunt—in letting Anne know that he was not happy with the way things were going. ["... the results on the quality project—at least at this point—aren't satisfactory." "I thought you were ready for taking on something bigger. But it doesn't seem to be working out."]

Being supportive: While he was candid in expressing his concerns about Anne's performance, he also continued to communicate his belief that she was capable and would be able to turn things around. ["... I haven't changed my mind that you can do this." "I believe you already have the talent and skills to make this project successful." "I want you to be successful and I'm sure that you can."]

Assigning responsibility: Tom made it clear that the project was not going well and that she was responsible. But instead of telling her what to do or how she should change, he asked her to come up with her own suggestions. ["Look, you're an engineer. A good one. You know how to figure things out." "I'll be happy to give you my own feedback, too, but I really expect you to take ownership of the project."]

Providing guidance: Tom heard Anne's suggestion about going to a project management training program and helped her see that attending a training program wasn't a viable solution to the problem. He coached her into coming up with better ideas. ["Let's think about the people you've known who have been really good team leaders. What did they do that you're not doing?"]

Earlier in the chapter I described the manager's role in coaching employees as giving *advice,* providing employees with *guidance,* providing employees with *support,* giving employees *confidence,* and helping employees gain greater *competence.* Each one of those coaching responsibilities was demonstrated in the conversation between Tom and Anne.

Finally, recognize that while it's possible that your feedback may not be 100 percent accurate, that's no excuse for not letting your people know how you feel they're doing.

Principles to Remember

DO

✓ Set a schedule for holding coaching sessions the same way you'd schedule a dentist's appointment.

✓ Allow people to make mistakes and learn from them.

✓ Conduct a formal midyear review in addition to informal coaching sessions.

DON'T

✓ Wait for a problem to arise to initiate a coaching session.

✓ Try to be a counselor when an individual is facing a personal problem.

✓ Confuse coaching with either training or disciplinary action.

Chapter **6**

Evaluating the Quality of an Individual's Performance

The process of evaluating performance begins during the performance planning meeting at the start of the review cycle when the manager discusses goals and key job responsibilities and competencies with each member of the team. In that discussion, along with talking about the results and behaviors expected, you and the subordinate need to talk about how the individual's performance will be measured and what you consider to be fully successful performance.

Note that your responsibility is to communicate clearly what Fully Successful or Meets Expectations performance looks like—the kind of performance that you consider to be worthy of a 3 rating on your company's 5-level rating scale. You shouldn't attempt to spell out what it will take to earn a rating of 5—Exceeds Expectations.

Here's why. Certainly every person in an organization would like to get a fully detailed answer to the always-asked question,

"What do I need to do to be considered an outstanding performer? What do I need to do to get a 5?" While managers frequently feel they ought to be able to answer this question, it is simply not possible to predict at the performance planning meeting what it will take to consider a person's job performance as Distinguished or Greatly Exceeds Expectations eleven months later when assessment time rolls around. Earning a superior rating is typically a function of innovation and creativity, of seeing an opportunity that no one else had noticed, or of discovering a more effective way to get a job done. These things can't be predicted in advance.

And that's OK. The manager doesn't have to spell out what the subordinate needs to do to earn the highest rating. If the manager is clear on the level of performance that he will consider as fully meeting expectations, or worthy of a 3 on a 5-level scale, then the variations from that level—positive or negative—will be obvious when the time comes for performance appraisal.

In addition to making clear what level of performance you consider to be fully successful, it's also useful at the start of the year to talk about how you plan to gather the information that you'll use to make the performance appraisal. For most items covered on the assessment form, you'll be able to evaluate the individual's performance simply by the results produced and your observation of the way the individual went about doing the job. But there may be areas where you'll need more information. For example, if customer service is a key component of the job, input from the employee's customers may be needed for an impartial assessment. How will the data from customers be collected? That's a good subject for you and the individual to talk about during the planning meeting. Don't wait until the end of the year to decide how to get the information.

Tracking Performance During the Year

After the performance planning meeting, you need to keep track of performance so that more than memory will be available when the time for appraisals comes around. Keeping a tracking system and requesting monthly reports are two techniques that managers have found useful.

A tracking system. Create a simple system for keeping track of events throughout the year. For example:

- A journal with tabs for each employee.

- A file on your computer dedicated to on-going performance notes (with a built-in reminder in your electronic calendar to enter notes on a regular basis).

- A hanging file with manila folders for keeping notes and copies of documents that reflect the quality of the employee's work or major projects the individual was involved in.

- E-mail folders set up for each person in the department, where copies of e-mails from both the manager and the individual can be placed for reference at appraisal-writing time.

- Finally, a very workable, low-tech solution: Brief, dated notes you store in a box or file.

Monthly reports. Another way to collect data is to ask each of your direct reports to send you a brief monthly report. The report might have four topic areas:

- Key accomplishments.

- Disappointments/concerns/problems.

- What will be accomplished next month.

- Suggestions to improve the department's effectiveness or the business as a whole.

In addition to being a valuable collection of source documents when you write the performance appraisal, the information contained in these monthly reports will provide the basis for effective coaching sessions and will alert you to problems that you might not be aware of. Further, the quality of the monthly reports submitted by each person, along with their completeness and timeliness, will give you useful information about how the person is doing the job.

The truth is that employees write their own reviews every day, when they come in to work promptly or late; finish a project well ahead of the deadline or miss it; volunteer to help a coworker learn a new software program; or avoid taking on any additional responsibilities. You merely serve as a journalist of sorts, documenting the day-to-day behavior and accomplishments of your staff.

The Need for Objectivity

Writing a person's performance appraisal, more than almost any other activity you perform as a manager, requires you to be fair, unprejudiced, and objective. But the fairness requirement does not mean that you can use only quantitative, numerical resources in completing the assessment. Your opinions, feelings, and judgments are what the appraisal process demands. Managers are paid to make judgments even when—or particularly when—all of the facts are not available. In every other area of managerial activity, the ability to act appropriately on the basis of limited and occasionally conflicting data is expected and rewarded. Only in the case of performance appraisal do we feel uncomfortable about the fact that nonquantitative and experienced-based information is used.

A false belief held by many people in organizations is that for a performance appraisal to be objective, there must be numerical, countable units to back up the assessments. That's simply not true.

"Objectivity" has nothing to do with quantifiability. It means to be uninfluenced by emotions or personal prejudices. It means to be fair. Objectivity has to do with being factual and basing appraisals on observable phenomena, like the way the person goes about performing his job.

Consider—how do you evaluate the performance of a pianist? By the number of notes she plays? How do you evaluate the performance of a painter? The number of pictures he paints or sells? Do you evaluate the performance of a priest by the number of confessions heard or the number of souls who gain entry to heaven (a valid measure perhaps, but accessing the data is problematic).

How do you evaluate the performance of a translator? The obvious, easy, and wrong answer: number of documents translated. But while that aspect of performance is easily quantified, it ignores what's genuinely important—the ability to capture nuance.

The ability to capture nuance isn't hard to evaluate accurately. Just take a document written in some foreign language and give it to two translators. Then take their two translations to a native speaker and ask, Which one got it right? The native speaker will read the two documents and then comfortably say, "This one translates each word accurately. But *this* one—this one captures what the writer really intended." That evaluation is certainly objective, but there's nothing quantifiable about it.

If you have access to numerical measures of the quantity of work the person did or have some quantitative index of quality to support your evaluation—terrific! Use them. But as long as you can provide solid examples to back up your assessments and ratings, then your appraisal is objective, even if you can't come up with countable units.

And even if some people mistakenly believe that without numbers to support it, your assessment is necessarily subjective, recognize that people desperately want this "subjective" information. People want to know their supervisor's opinion of their work. They want honest answers to their most important questions: How am I doing? Are you pleased with my performance? Do I have a bright future here? There is no number that can answer those questions.

Fewer jobs today produce the kind of quantifiable results that lead to easy evaluation. The outputs of knowledge workers are harder to assess than those of widget makers. Even in P&L positions, where results are clear and performance seems easily quantifiable, just making your numbers is no longer enough. Companies demand not only results, but insist that people generate those results in a way that reflects organizational values. GE and PepsiCo, two companies famous for decades of attention to performance management, are good examples of this dual focus on both results and behavior. When he was CEO of PepsiCo, Wayne Calloway said, "It's easy to get fired from PepsiCo. You'll get fired if you don't make your numbers. You'll get fired if you lie. And the fastest way to get fired is to lie about your numbers."[1]

After its Session C forced-ranking assessments that caught so much flak several years ago, GE today has moved away from the harsh "Fire the bottom 10 percent!" approach the company used when Jack Welch was CEO. But GE is clear about what's important, as demonstrated by its statement, from a presentation given by a GE HR executive several years ago: "Values must accompany demonstrated operational excellence in order to advance." In GE's Session Cs today, managers are assessed along two dimensions: performance and values. Low performance but a strong demonstration of GE's values produces an assessment of "Restart: Second Opportunity to Deliver Results." But if you deliver high performance with low adherence to values? "Remove: Removals Reinforce Importance of Values Dimension."

Although the results an individual produces may be quantifiable, how she got those results, and the extent to which she modeled the organization's values in generating them, isn't subject to numerical measure. But behavior and adherence to values can certainly be described, and those descriptions of performance, supported by examples, are certainly objective.

Recognize too that some performance measures may be quantifiable, but are more trouble to get than they're worth. For example, one list of sample HR performance measures recommends tracking such items as number of days to answer suggestions, average time a visitor spends in the lobby, percentage of personnel problems handled by the employee's manager, and turnover rate due to poor performance. Certainly it's important that suggestions receive timely responses, and that visitors are greeted quickly. But is it really worth counting the number of days that a suggestion waits for an answer, or putting a stopwatch to visitor-greeting performance? It's unlikely that it will be possible to collect the data on the number of problems solved in a department without coming to HR's attention. Finally, while it may be possible to calculate the turnover rate due to poor performance, is a low turnover rate good or bad?

Albert Einstein is credited with the insight that best makes the point: "Not everything that counts can be counted. And not everything that can be counted counts."

Making the Assessment

If you approach the appraisal writing process with certain beliefs and assumptions, you will have little difficulty in generating an appraisal that is fair, unprejudiced, and objective. Keep these assumptions in mind:

- The purpose of the performance appraisal is to further the organization's purposes by strengthening the performance of every member of the organization.

- You will never have "all the facts" and in spite of that you must still do the job.

- The bar is rising every year, and what was good enough last year is no longer good enough this year.

- People genuinely want to know what their boss thinks of their performance.

- People are capable of handling the truth about their performance, even when that truth is unpleasant.

- It is better to set the performance bar high and demand more of people than to settle for whatever level of performance they choose to give.

- The ability and willingness of any given individual to perform is unrelated to that individual's race, sex, religion, or any other non-job-related factor.[2]

To start the assessment process, gather all your materials that provide information on the quality of the individual's work, including your notes from the initial goal-setting meeting. Review the goals and update the status for each. Which goals have been completed, which ones abandoned because of a higher priority or a shift in business focus? For each of the employee's key job responsibilities, marshal the data that will support whatever appraisal rating you decide to give.

Start with the Job, Not with the Person

When a manager completes a performance appraisal of an individual, he's not assessing the quality of the person. He is evaluating how well this individual performed this particular job.

Reread the job description and ask yourself some questions that will bring the job into clear focus:

- The reason the company created this job is to

  _____.

- The most important ways a person doing the job should spend time are _____.

- The two or three most important duties of someone in this position are _____.

- If someone asked me what it takes to be successful in this job, I would say, _____.

- The easiest way to determine whether this job is being done well is by _____.

Questions like these have nothing to do with the performance of the specific individual doing the job. They deal with the job itself. Answering these questions helps give you a standard by which to compare the employee's performance with what you and the organization as a whole expect to get for your investment. Before you can ask, "How well is the person doing?" you need to determine what it is you want to get done.

Assessing the Individual

While ranking employees against each other is unlikely to be part of your company's performance appraisal procedure, it's an effective way for you to get perspective when you begin the evaluation process. Of all the people on your team, who's the best? Who else is right up there with her? Who's in the middle of your pack? Who lags behind the rest? How far back do they lag?

Following are some criteria and questions to ask that will both generate the information needed to accurately assess the quality of an individual's performance and highlight areas where the manager needs to collect more data:[3]

- **Ambition/initiative:** Does the employee demonstrate ambition in the position (not to move out of it, but to perform it) and take initiative to improve the process, product, and overall work environment?

- **Attendance:** Has the employee's attendance (even if it is within your company's guidelines) had a negative impact on the department productivity or morale? Has the employee's attendance been exemplary?

- **Attitude/cooperation:** What is the employee's attitude toward you, toward peers, toward the work and the world in general? Is he or she a pleasure or a chore to work with? Is the employee reasonably flexible when asked to perform a job function outside his or her normal duties, or to work outside his or her normal hours for a special project?

- **Communication skills:** Does the employee have the ability to adequately communicate with peers, managers, and customers? Have any issues been created—or solved—due to the employee's communication skills?

- **Department and company oriented:** Does the employee have a broader view and deeper understanding beyond simply his or her own duties? Does he or she speak of the department or company with pride?

- **Focus:** Is the employee able to maintain focus on the task at hand? Does he or she have difficulty prioritizing job duties above personal business or socializing with other employees?

- **Improvement from previous evaluation:** Has the employee demonstrated marked improvement from the previous performance evaluation?

- **Integrity:** Does the employee demonstrate ethical behavior in the workplace? Does he or she respect the privacy of other employees and of customers?

- **Knows when to ask:** Is the employee able to differentiate between independence and arrogance in the performance of job duties? Does he or she know when to ask a question rather than simply making a guess and moving on?

- **Level of technical knowledge:** Does the employee have and demonstrate an acceptable level of technical knowledge to perform his or her job duties? Do other people seek this individual out when they run into problems?

- **Productivity/deadlines:** Is the employee able to consistently meet productivity requirements and project deadlines?

- **Quality of work:** Has there been positive or negative feedback from customers regarding the quality of the employee's work? What have you observed regarding the employee's work quality?

- **Reliability/go-to person:** Is the employee reliable? Does he or she consistently demonstrate competence and dependability? Is he or she your "go-to" person?

- **Stress management:** How does the employee deal with changes in the work environment? Is he or she able to filter out the noise and focus on the task at hand in order to complete it on time? How does the employee interact with other members of the department when tensions are high?

- **Teamwork/pitching in:** If the department is short-handed, does the employee willingly pitch in to finish tasks assigned to others, where appropriate? Does the employee volunteer to assist?

Is Self-Appraisal a Good Idea?

Asking the employee to write a self-appraisal using the company's appraisal form might seem to be an effective technique. Many management books and articles recommend a self-appraisal, including having the employee give himself a rating. An employee's self-appraisal might give the manager valuable data on the quality of an individual's performance as well as a preview of what might be expected when the two sit down to review the manager's performance appraisal. It would seem to be a good idea.

It's not a good idea. It's a bad idea and needs to be stomped out.

Here's why. Research consistently demonstrates that individuals are notoriously inaccurate in assessing their own performance, and the poorer the performer, the higher (and more inaccurate) the self-assessment. Research by the consulting firm Lominger, Inc. indicates that "the overall correlation between self-ratings and performance was .00. The most accurate rater by far is the immediate boss."[4]

In their well-known article, "Unskilled and Unaware of It: How Difficulties in Recognizing One's Own Incompetence Lead to Inflated Self-Assessments," Cornell University researchers Justin Kruger and David Dunning report that those who are incompetent performers are also incapable of assessing the difference between good and bad performance.[5] As they put it, "When people are incompetent in the strategies they adopt to achieve success and satisfaction, they suffer a dual burden: Not only do they reach erroneous conclusions and make unfortunate choices, but their incompetence robs them of the ability to realize it. Instead, they are left with the mistaken impression that they are doing just fine."

One senior executive describing his company's experience using a forced-ranking procedure to identify its A, B, and C performers told me of the same problem: "The As are afraid they'll be considered Bs, the Bs are scared they'll be seen as Cs, and all the Cs are convinced that they're A players."

In July 2007 *BusinessWeek* surveyed two thousand Americans in middle management positions and above, asking them the question, "Are you one of the top 10% of performers in your company?" Not one of the subgroups in the survey had less than 80 percent of the respondents answer the question affirmatively. Eighty-four percent of all middle managers reported that they were in the top 10 percent of performers in their company. Among executives—the most deluded cluster by far—97 percent of those who were asked whether they were in the top 10 percent group answered yes.[6]

Here's the most serious problem with asking an employee to write a self-appraisal. By doing so you may create a false impression of what the nature of performance appraisal is. When he's asked to write a self-appraisal, particularly when the company's appraisal form is used, it's easy for an employee to assume that the structure of the performance appraisal process is that both the individual and the boss separately write their appraisals of the individual's performance. They then get together, share each one's document with the other, and come to a common agreement on the final appraisal.

That's wrong. Again, the appraisal is a record of *the supervisor's opinion*. The review meeting is a discussion, not a negotiation. Asking the individual to write a self-appraisal encourages misunderstanding by both parties.

An Alternative to Self-Appraisal

If company policy dictates that employees be asked (or ordered) to write self-appraisals, company policy must be followed. But the manager can prevent much of the mischief just described by explaining to his team exactly what the purpose of the self-appraisal is (a way to gain information from the employee's point of view) and how it will be used (as a data source for the supervisor in preparing the actual performance appraisal). It's wise to ask the employee to submit the self-appraisal to the supervisor well in advance of the performance appraisal discussion so that the supervisor can use the data as an input to the official appraisal and not wait until the review meeting to find out what the employee has written. Finally, it helps to refer to the document the employee is preparing as the "self-assessment" while the document produced by the supervisor is the "official performance appraisal."

However, it is valuable to get information from the individual to help the manager create a well-rounded, complete, and objective appraisal, even if writing a self-appraisal on a blank copy of the company's form isn't the best approach. A more effective approach is for the supervisor, at the start of performance appraisal season, to ask each direct report to send him an informal list of his or her most important accomplishments and achievements during the appraisal period. The list can be e-mailed or written on a blank piece of paper—there's no official form. And nothing needs to be said about any problems or shortcomings or failures that occurred. The manager's purpose is to make sure that none of the employee's successes are overlooked.

This "good stuff" list will provide the same value as a formal self-appraisal and will help remove some of the negativity that surrounds many people's feelings about the performance appraisal process.

Rating Errors

Finally, the manager needs to be aware of the existence of rating errors as he goes about assessing the quality of the individual's performance. Most managers are familiar with the most common ones: *Central Tendency* (rating everyone in the middle of the rating scale), *Halo/Horns Effect* (letting one aspect of an individual's performance influence unrelated areas of that person's evaluation), *Similar-to-Me Effect* (the tendency of individuals to rate people who resemble themselves more highly than they rate others), and perhaps the most common, *Recency Effect* (the tendency for recent minor events to have more influence on the rating than major events of many months ago).

Then there's the *Hired or Inherited* issue. More than two decades ago, research done by Professor David Schoorman showed that whether or not the supervisor had hired or inherited her employees was a better predictor of evaluation results than actual job performance. Employees hired by people doing the reviews got higher scores because of the greater psychological commitment managers have to the people they put themselves on the line to hire.[7]

One final rating error that can unconsciously influence an appraiser's assessment of an individual is the *Attractiveness Effect*—the well-documented tendency for people to assume that those who are physically attractive are also superior performers. If a manager has a Julia Roberts and a Golda Meir on his team, it wouldn't be surprising if the manager rates Julia higher, even though there's no difference at all in the quality of their performance. Consultant Susan Webber observes, "Like it or not, prevailing social preferences are replicated in the corporate world. Height is correlated with greater starting salaries and greater likelihood of becoming CEO. Pretty people are better paid."[8] They may be better appraised, too.

Principles to Remember

DO

✓ Start by thinking about the *job,* not the *person.*

✓ Keep an ongoing record of each individual's performance during the year.

✓ Compare each individual's performance with the performance of everyone else on the team.

DON'T

✓ Try to tell people what they must do to get the highest appraisal rating.

✓ Feel that your appraisal isn't objective just because it's based on your opinion.

✓ Set your performance expectations at a level anyone can achieve—make them tough and demanding.

Chapter 7

Using Your Appraisal Form

Now that you've assessed how well the individual performed during the review period, it's time to transfer your judgments of the individual's performance to your company's appraisal form.

The first step is to figure out how effectively the form you're using allows you to appraise performance. Every appraisal of an individual requires considering two components: behaviors and results. Does the form your company provides allow you to appropriately describe and evaluate both what the person accomplished and how she went about doing the job? Or is it merely a trait list with check boxes for each trait? Is it a totally unstructured essay format? Or is it entirely results focused, asking how well the individual met the goals assigned but allowing no space for discussing the way the person went about achieving those goals?

The more inadequate the form, the more latitude you probably have to adjust it to meet your needs. If your company's performance appraisal form is poorly constructed, the chances are good that you've got room to repair the faults in the system. If the criteria for the appraisal are lax, vague, or insufficiently job re-lated, you can start with those criteria but redefine them for your department in a concrete, job-specific way. Managers typically have a great deal of discretion in informing subordinates about their performance to let people know where they stand, to recognize excellence, and to generate performance improvements.

You can often overcome problems with deficient forms by attaching additional documentation. For example, including a list of the employee's goals that were determined at the start of the year along with an assessment of performance can shore up a solely traits-based form. And a similar document that concentrates on performance against competencies can provide needed information when the form itself asks only about goal achievement.

You don't have to wait until evaluation time to upgrade a less-than-perfect performance appraisal system. There's no reason why you can't correct shortcomings in the process at any time during the year by conducting a midcycle goal-setting session or by getting your team together to discuss the performance appraisal process and how it will work in your department from now on. The point is this—it's never too late to demonstrate performance appraisal excellence, and the right time to start is right now.

Understanding Your Company's Form

Before you begin to assess an individual's performance on your company's appraisal form, make sure you understand how it operates. Review it to make sure that it allows for all important areas of performance to be assessed. Make note of where you can best discuss and rate various aspects of the individual's performance. Some things to consider:

Does the form cover both behavior and results? If the form doesn't allow for evaluating both dimensions of performance—behavior and results—consider adding a supplementary sheet to cover whatever's missing. If that's not workable, there's probably a narrative section at the end for final observations and comments you can use.

Does the form provide a specific section for goals? It's vital to include the assessment of performance against goals. If a goals section is missing, consider including a separate narrative with assessments of performance against each goal.

Does the form give you space for comments, both on individual items and in a final summary? The rationale for a rating is often more important than the rating itself, since that explanation provides the context for the rating. It's rare to find a performance appraisal form that provides no space for narrative or comments. If that space is limited to summary comments at the end of the form, use it to fully explain your rationale for the rating you assigned to the most important items.

What rating scale does the form use? Almost every performance appraisal form uses a 3-level, 4-level, or 5-level scale. Later in this chapter I'll discuss how to use these effectively.

Are labels provided? Most appraisal forms, in addition to a numerical rating scale, have a rating label for each level. Whatever the terminology your form may use, let people know what the words mean to you. For example, your form may provide a 3-level rating scale with the conventional labels Fails to Meet Expectations, Meets Expectations, and Exceeds Expectations. It's wise to tell people well before the day of their performance review that as far as you're concerned, Meets Expectations means that the individual consistently demonstrated a high level of execution and from time to time did even more. Explain that, to you, Exceeds Expectations is the rating you'll use to recognize those who have performed in an exemplary way in all areas of their job, with respect to both competencies and results. And while even the poorest performer doesn't totally fail to meet expectations in every aspect of job performance, tell your staff you'll be using the Fails to Meet Expectations rating whenever a core part of an individual's job has not been performed at a fully successful level. It's better to have this conversation, and deal with the questions and quarrels people will have about how their performance will be rated, when there's not yet a rating attached and the discussion is intended only to generate understanding, not to explain or justify a particular rating.

Are there guidelines on the form (or in the policy) about the distribution of appraisal ratings? More than half of all *Fortune* 500 companies provide a recommended or required distribution of performance appraisal ratings.

Does the form provide space for employee comments? It should. Most do. If yours doesn't, invite the employee to write a document summarizing his or her response (and, perhaps, rejoinder) to your official performance appraisal.

Does the form include a section on development, or is that a separate (or nonexistent) procedure? Development is usually considered part of performance management, but it's rare that a person's successes or failures in completing a development plan are factored in to determine the final rating.

Writing Comments

The rule is simple: state your assessment and support it with facts and examples.

You don't have to use all of your examples on the performance appraisal form. Use the most telling illustrations, particularly if you're dealing with an area of predictable sensitivity (like commenting on less-than-perfect performance in the ethics and integrity competency) or one where your perception of the quality of an individual's performance differs from his (like the quality of customer service provided). Save the other examples to further support your appraisal judgment if this becomes a point of contention during the review.

Once you've stated your assessment of the individual's performance, either for a specific assessment item or in your summary comments, then concentrate on the specific data that support the judgment you've made. Your model is Joe Friday, the cop in the 1950s TV series *Dragnet*. Whenever Friday was faced with a citizen who started to pour her heart out in response to his request for information about a crime, he'd interrupt with, "Just the facts, ma'am." That's your job—to provide just the facts that support your evaluation.

Throw away phrase books that give boilerplate comments, and be cautious about using the text-generator feature built into many online systems. With phrase books, you'll spend far more time trying to track down precisely the right phrase to describe someone's performance than if you just write your comment based simply on what you've observed. One of the deceptively bad features of many Web-based appraisal systems is their ability to generate comments and phrases that are advertised as tailored directly to the rating level that the manager clicks. One of these systems offers even more bells and whistles: its "Comment Helper" includes a "Nuance Button" that supposedly allows a manager to make the machine-generated text for a 3 or any other rating just a teeny bit more positive or negative.

These books and electronic text generators are not to be trusted. Their offerings are either insipid or so generic as to be worthless. (One book offers such distinctive phrases as "Sets priorities well," "Misses important deadlines," "Thorough, reliable, and accurate.") Even the dullest employee can spot language that was generated by a "Comment Writer" or lifted verbatim out of a book of a thousand phrases.

Remember, appraising someone's performance requires you to be judgmental. Can you be judgmental and still be objective? Yes, as long as your comments are about behaviors and not about the character of the person himself. If you would have the same judgment no matter whose behavior it was (including your own), if your intention is to promote learning and have the individual succeed, if you've talked with the individual about your expectations and provided a clear description of excellence, and if you've supported your judgment with facts and observations, then you are an objective appraiser who is rendering an objective judgment.

How to Use a 3-, 4-, and 5-Level Rating Scale

Most performance appraisal systems use three, four, or five levels to rate performance. There are some systems that use a two-level (pass/fail) approach. There are some that use seven or nine (or even more) levels, and some that have no final rating. These are rare. The majority of organizations in America, Europe, and Asia use a five-level system.

Using a 3-Level Scale

A 3-level rating scale is the second most popular type of rating scale. It's a distant runner-up to the 5-level scale, the most common scale used in performance appraisal.

In a 3-level scale, the distribution of scores will probably be 10 percent 1s, 70 percent 2s, and 20 percent 3s. While this distribution recognizes that twice as many people exceed the manager's expectations than fail to meet those expectations, a score range of 1–3 is just too narrow. This is partly because life just isn't that simple, but mainly because the middle option encourages fence-sitting, which inhibits clarity of communication. The individual who is just barely into the 2–Meets Expectations category (the person, say, whose performance is at the 15th percentile) ends up with the same 2 rating as the person at the 75th percentile of performance. But the first person is much closer to those whose lackluster performance earned the bottom 1–Fails to Meet Expectations rating than she is to her colleague at the 70th percentile, whose performance is almost into the 3–Exceeds Expectations category. Three-level scales can provide differentiation between those whose performance is at the bottom of the barrel and those who are genuinely top performers, but they can't make any gradations among the great majority of people who are somewhere in the middle, even though the relative performance of some of these people is significantly better than that of the rest.

One of the cures when your appraisal form offers only three rating levels is to think about what each of the three levels really means, regardless of the official labels attached to the scale. Instead of thinking about whether the individual Fails to Meet/ Meets/Exceeds, it's more productive to think of the labels as representing Occasionally Meets, Consistently Meets/Sometimes Exceeds, and Routinely Exceeds.

Using a 4-Level Scale

The supposed benefit of the 4-level rating scale (or any rating scale with an even number of positions) is that there is no position in the center, thus eliminating the possibility of the appraiser's rating everyone in the middle. Of course, this good intention rarely produces the desired result.

The 4-level rating scale used by most companies (there aren't many) usually provides one negative rating, one neutral rating (the equivalent of 3–Meets Expectations), and two positive ratings. In effect, a 4-level scale is just a 5-level scale that's had the lowest level deleted.

The most effective way to use a 4-level scale is to make believe it's a 5-level scale with the *top level* removed. Since no one wants to be rated as below average, which a rating of 2 on a 4-level scale would certainly communicate even if the label says otherwise, assume that the 3 on a 4-level scale represents the same quality of performance as a 3 on a 5-level scale. Then, instead of having two categories in which to place superior performers, the manager has only one. The bottom level, as is true with virtually any rating scale, will probably be used only in rare instances.

Thus, whatever labels the company provides, the actual use of the 4-level scale by the manager will reflect the following descriptions of an individual's performance:

1. Completely Unsatisfactory/Unacceptable

2. Needs Improvement/Change for the Better Required

3. Meets Expectations/Fully Successful/Good Solid Performer

4. Superior/Outstanding/Distinguished

Using a 5-Level Scale

The 5-level rating scale is by far the most common in organizations in the United States and around the world.

The reason a 5-level scale is so popular is that most managers believe (probably accurately) that they can discriminate among five levels of performance: the truly unacceptable; that which is in need of improvement; the fully successful; superior performance; and finally that which is genuinely distinguished. Since managers can recognize five levels of performance, and since five levels allows for sufficient discrimination to make valid personnel decisions in areas like compensation, promotions, and layoffs, a 5-level scale is probably the wisest choice. In fact, offering more than five rating levels actually tends to reduce the amount of differentiation rather than increase it.

Companies routinely provide labels and definitions for each of the five rating levels, but these don't usually offer managers much help. Let's look at how a 5-level scale operates, along with the conventional label set.

1–Unsatisfactory.   The dilemma faced by managers in using the 1 rating is that this level is so stigmatizing that it is almost never used. Only if the manager discovers that he has the organizational equivalent of an ax murderer or terrorist working for him will he use the absolute bottom of the scale. Even then he's likely to look for some aspect of the person's performance to rate sufficiently high ("charismatic leadership," perhaps) so that the final rating won't have to be the disgraceful 1. Thus the 1 rating on a 5-level scale too often serves as a false bottom.

But in any group of twenty people, there's almost always going to be one whose performance lags far behind all the rest. That's the person—one out of twenty, or 5 percent—for whom you should use the 1 rating.

2–Needs Improvement.   There are two entirely different circumstances that justify the use of the 2 rating. The first is the individual who simply isn't doing a very good job and needs to shape up immediately. The other is the person who is newly hired or promoted into the position and, while on track, is not yet at a fully successful level of performance.

Several companies provide managers with a form that allows them to distinguish between these two situations. John Deere solved the problem neatly by providing an opt-out rating labeled "On Target" to identify those people whose performance trajectory is exactly where it should be, but who aren't yet fully proficient.

But what do you do if you have a fairly new, "on-target" individual on your team whose performance isn't yet quite up to level 3, there's no opt-out rating offered, and the performance appraisal rating tightly governs the amount of the individual's merit increase? In a case like this, the wisest thing to do is to rate the person a 3 (thus not hurting the person financially) while being clear in the appraisal narrative that while the person is indeed on target, the target itself has not yet been reached.

If the manager and her organization have tough and demanding performance standards, 15 to 20 percent of all employees should expect to get a 2 rating.

3–Meets Expectations/Fully Successful/Good Solid Performer. This is the rating level that provides the best assessment of the performance of half to two-thirds of the people in an organization. But there are problems with using the middle rating. First, nobody wants to be thought of as run-of-the-mill, average, or mediocre—a C student. One way to break through this mistaken mind-set is to describe the 3 level on your performance appraisal form as representing the equivalent of par in golf—the level of play expected of an expert (acknowledging that there are still birdies and eagles available for the few who are able to break par).

Another dilemma is that a lot of people equate simply showing up regularly and doing exactly what they're told as meeting expectations, and therefore any performance that's even slightly better than that should be recognized with a least a 4 rating. This person will argue correctly that during the course of the year she performed with excellence, solved problems, and was innovative. (Thus, "Gimme a 4!") But performing with excellence, problem solving, and finding ways to do the job cheaper/faster/better are expected in all positions in a company. Do that and you earn a 3 rating—you met the manager's and the organization's expectations. ("Here's your 3.") Explaining this at the start of the year can preclude grandiose expectations.

4–Exceeds Expectations/Superior/Above Standard. This is the appropriate performance rating for 20 to 30 percent of the employees in an organization. Since firms don't hire people at random but select and promote the best talent available, expecting strict adherence to a normal distribution curve is unfounded. In most cases there will be about twice as many people who get a rating one level higher than the middle one than those who get a rating one level lower.

5–Greatly Exceeds Expectations/Distinguished/Outstanding. Just like the 1 rating, the 5 rating is underused. In the next section we'll look at using the 1 and 5 ratings for maximum performance management payoff.

Using the Extremes of the Rating Scale

There are advantages and disadvantages for each alternative to the number of rating levels. However, a consistent problem is that appraisers rarely use all of the levels available to them, no matter how many may be offered.

The 1 Rating

If managers are setting tough and demanding performance standards and are telling the truth in their written appraisals, around 5 percent of the staff should expect to get the lowest rating. But awarding a staff member a well-deserved 1 on a company's performance appraisal rating scale isn't easy. Consultant Susan Webber makes the point well: "There are considerable barriers to a manager giving his staff member honest and useful feedback that lead to inflated reviews. They both have an on-going relationship; and thus both sides do not want the review process to create friction. Yet most employees have an inflated view of their own achievements, which predisposes them to doubt, perhaps even resent, a truthful appraisal. And since the assessment of a job of any complexity is largely subjective, it's difficult for the boss to defend a rating that is at odds with the employee's self-assessment. In addition, managers consider themselves at least partly responsible for their subordinate's performance. Thus a low rating reflects badly on them."[1]

Recently I got a call from a woman who had been a participant in a management seminar on performance appraisal that I had conducted for her company. She was writing her appraisal of a poor performer, and was on the fence about whether to use the 1 rating that the quality of both the employee's work and attitude demanded, or to soften the blow with a 2 rating.

I asked her the "Ann Landers question." Ann Landers, a popular advice columnist from the 1970s to the 1990s, would always respond with the same question whenever an unhappy wife asked Ann's opinion about whether she should get a divorce from her husband. Ann's question: "Are you better off with him or without him?"

I asked her the same question about her employee. "Without him," she responded without hesitation. Give him the 1, I told her. Not only will it make termination easier since the employee has been clearly told that his performance is unsatisfactory, the company can also demonstrate that the individual had been plainly put on record about his poor performance in the event of any legal challenge.

Failing to give the poor performer the blunt 1 rating that his performance deserves is doing a disservice to both the individual and the company. Inflated appraisals result in the organization's being stuck with a cadre of mediocre performers. Organizational deadwood proliferates. Worse, when the organization finally does realize the need to cut loose noncontributors and begins removing those whose contribution is marginal, it will be haunted by a history of above-average appraisals given to below-average performers. The fear of wrongful-termination litigation may then cause the organization to act far more slowly than it should.

The employee who has been awarded an appraisal rating higher than he actually deserves is being done no kindness either. The status quo will continue, the performance will remain unchanged, and the employee is likely to be either passed over for opportunities he might have had if he had received honest feedback about the need for change and acted on it, or promoted to a job he can't handle. Short-term kindheartedness—the supervisor's reluctance to straightforwardly identify and discuss performance shortcomings—may produce long-term harm to the deficient performer.

The 5 Rating

As reluctant as managers are to assign a truly noncontributing member of the team a well-deserved 1 rating, I find managers equally reluctant to award a 5. In some companies this is caused by the compensation system's putting arbitrary limits on the number of high ratings that can be awarded. But it may also result from a manager's reluctance to stick her neck out too far. She knows that with her star performer, she'll run into no opposition when her performance appraisal rating is a 4, but will face serious scrutiny if she decides to give that star performer the 5 his performance has really earned. This reluctance represents a lack of courage rather than a system failure. The cure is for that nervous manager's boss to say, "Marie, all year long you've told me that Donald does work that is genuinely remarkable. But you haven't used the 5 rating in his performance appraisal? Why not?"

Just hearing that statement from her boss may give the manager the guts needed to recognize a top performer with the appraisal system's top rating. But the manager may have other fears about using the top of the rating scale. One is that the top-talent individual, having been awarded a 5, will now feel grandfathered in to that rating and will slack off since continued 5s are assured. There is no evidence of this, and plenty of reports contradict this idea. The top performer, having discovered that excellent performance actually is recognized, is likely to crank the engine even higher since he has discovered that peak performance is noticed and rewarded.

A person doesn't earn a 5 rating by generating a breathtakingly high level of superlative performance every week over a full fifty-two-week period. A more appropriate rationale for rating someone a 5 is that the person performed his job all year at a superior level (i.e., at a level of performance that would justify a 4 rating), and, in addition, had one particularly successful project or achievement during the year. The next year the person's performance might continue at the same superior level, but without any special project or unique accomplishment. In this case the employee's performance would be rightly evaluated with a 4 rating. The 4 would not indicate a decline in the person's overall performance; rather, it would reflect the fact that in the preceding year, the person successfully pulled off a big-deal project. This year no such project was on his menu. It's logical to expect that, if the performance appraisal system is running right, there will be a significant amount of churn in the people who earn 5s from year to year.

Remember, a performance appraisal rating represents a unique assessment of the quality of an individual's performance over a specific twelve-month period. It is not a lifetime achievement award.

Finally, the wise manager always preps her boss when it looks like a 1 or a 5 rating will be awarded to one of her subordinates, or any other rating that the manager feels may take her boss by surprise.

Determining the Final Rating

The most challenging requirement of the performance appraisal process may be determining your final rating of the individual's overall performance, particularly if this task is a function of managerial judgment (as it should be) and not merely the mathematical calculation of a final rating by averaging all the individual ratings on the form. If your performance appraisal system generates a final rating for you based solely on averaging all of your individual item ratings without further managerial input, your job is done. But you'll probably discover that most of the final ratings the system calculates will be between 3.4 and 3.6. Since most people's ratings therefore will be pretty much the same, you'll need to use the comments section to communicate exactly how you see the quality of each individual's performance.

Most appraisal systems allow for some managerial discretion; the best require managers to make the final call based on their judgment of the individual's overall performance over the course of the year. If your system allows you to assign the final rating, consider the following ways to come up with the most accurate assessment.

First, review all the individual-item ratings you have made in the body of the appraisal. While the final rating does not have to equal the mathematical sum of all of the individual ratings in the form, there should be a reasonable consistency between the individual ratings and the final rating. Only when one performance factor was performed so well or so poorly that it overshadowed all the others should one factor have an outsized influence on the final result.

Also, consider informally weighting the various parts of the appraisal. If your form or procedure already provides for predetermined weights, then this part of the job has already been done for you. The best performance appraisal procedures, however, leave the option of assigning weights up to the manager. If no weights are specifically assigned or required by the form, you can, for example, simply decide to allocate one-third of your overall performance rating to how well the individual did in the competencies portion and two-thirds to how well he achieved his work goals.

Whatever weighting system you decide will provide the most accurate picture of a subordinate's performance, be sure to let people know well in advance of the appraisal so that that they can put their efforts where you are expecting successes.

Using Distribution Guidelines

A solid body of research data confirms that there is a significant difference in the contributions made by employees performing at outstanding, fully satisfactory, and marginal levels. Most managers agree that there is a significant variation in the quality of performance among members of a work group. Most non-supervisory employees agree.

But we also know that managers are reluctant to use the extremes of their rating scale. In addition, many organizations build disincentives to honest assessment directly into the system itself. For example, if the performance appraisal system tightly links the amount of the individual's salary increase with her rating on the performance appraisal form, managers will be tugged between honesty and generosity. When gasoline and grocery prices are at record highs, managers understandably want to be generous with their team members. To do so, they may decide to artificially inflate a rating to bump up a merit increase.

As a result, it is a fairly common practice among large and well-managed organizations in America to provide guidelines or targets for the expected distribution of performance appraisal ratings. (Providing distribution guidelines, particularly with required or forced distributions, is less common in European and Asian organizations.) The purpose of such guidelines is to assure that differences in the quality of performance between individuals is reflected in their appraisal ratings.

I explained earlier that it's *not* appropriate to expect performance appraisal ratings to distribute themselves normally according to an exact bell-shaped or normal distribution curve, since organizations are not composed of a random collection of individuals. It's appropriate to expect a somewhat positive skew in performance appraisal results.

Whirlpool Corporation is one of many organizations that publishes their distribution guidelines. Their guidelines reflect the company's intentional positive skew:[2]

Extraordinary Results	5%
Very Strong Results	20%
Strong Results	60%
Results Need to Be Improved	10%
Unacceptable Results	5%

But faced with a set of distribution guidelines and a small number of subordinates, managers are likely to seek exception from the requirement that the guidelines be followed precisely. If the manager has only four subordinates, for example, it seems unfair to require strict guideline adherence. In fact, companies that provide distribution guidelines often encourage rating inflation with statements like, "These guidelines are the type of distribution you should find when looking at large groups (for example, 200 or more employees). You would not expect to find this distribution in a small group of 5 to 25 employees." Managers will accept this statement as permission to vary from the guidelines (always on the high side) for their small group of direct reports.

If the guidelines rigidly apply, one solution to the small-population problem is the use of calibration sessions to increase the number of people to whom the guidelines apply. I discuss calibration in the next chapter. If your company doesn't use calibration sessions, then the wisest approach is to come as close as you can to the published guidelines. If your distributions vary from the requirements, develop a strong business case to support why the results that your unit achieved justify an exemption from those guidelines.

Dealing with Rating Quotas

In some cases, limits are set on the number of high ratings because the performance appraisal system is driven by the compensation system. A manager may be told that he must limit the number of people who get a 4 or a 5 rating "because there's not enough money in the salary budget." This is a case of reversed priorities, with the number of high ratings determined not by the quality of people's performance but by the amount of money available for salary increases. It is just as workable to have the performance appraisal system drive the compensation system. In this case, when performance appraisals are complete, the final ratings are reviewed to assure accuracy (not compliance with the salary budget). Once the ratings at the various levels have been determined, it is then easy to allocate whatever the budget may be for increases to make sure that those who are highest rated get the lion's share of the money.

But that's not a problem the individual manager can solve. If you are forced to adjust a rating downward because the compensation system limits the number of high ratings, make your case for awarding the rating that most accurately reflects your assessment of the individual's performance. If you're refused, stop. You made your point. You were overruled. And whatever you do, don't whine to your employee during your performance appraisal discussion, "I had you in for a higher rating, but the people above me forced me to move it down because they say there's not enough money in the budget for me to give you the rating you really deserve." That's contemptible. Grow up. Deal with it. Move on.

Principles to Remember

DO

✓ Evaluate both behaviors and results.

✓ Let everyone know that the middle rating represents shooting par, not run-of-the-mill or mediocre performance.

✓ Use the extremes of your rating scale to rate performance that is unsatisfactory or outstanding.

DON'T

✓ Be constrained by the format of the form—adapt it so you can tell the whole story.

✓ Use performance appraisal phrase books or online appraisal systems' text-generating features to write your
   comments.

✓ Come up with the final rating by approaching it as an
   arithmetic problem.

Chapter 8

Preparing for the Appraisal Discussion

You've written the individual's performance appraisal and determined a rating. But how do you know the rating you've decided on is correct?

We all remember from our school days that some teachers were hard graders and others were easy. The same is true in organizations. There are managers who—if left unchecked—will rate every subordinate as Exceeds Expectations. But performance evaluations and ratings impact directly on compensation, promotions, succession planning, and talent management. There's too much at stake to allow erroneous ratings to paint a distorted picture of organizational talent.

Calibration Sessions and Reviewer Requirements

In the past several years, organizations around the world have become more concerned with rating accuracy and driving the truth into performance appraisal. In addition to providing guidelines for the distribution of appraisal ratings, as discussed in the last chapter, companies are also adopting the use of calibration sessions and imposing reviewer requirements to increase appraisal accuracy.

Calibration Sessions

The use of calibration procedures has been growing dramatically since they were developed about ten years ago. When I wrote about calibration sessions in 2005, about a third of all major organizations were using them.[1] Today, my informal polls indicate that 60 to 70 percent of large organizations are using calibration (or "rater-reliability" or "leveling") sessions.

Here's how they work. Supervisors first write preliminary performance appraisals, including proposed ratings, for each of their team members. Groups of supervisors then meet and post for everyone else in the meeting to see the ratings they are planning to assign each of their employees. Each supervisor explains the rationale behind his proposed ratings and also examines the proposed appraisal ratings posted by his peers. He listens to his colleagues' inputs and recommendations. The supervisor then makes adjustments, up or down, if he finds that his ratings are out of sync with the standards set by the others in the session. When everyone's ratings have been reviewed and all adjustments have been made, the meeting ends and the ratings become official.

Calibration meetings help assure consistency in ratings. They reduce rating errors and increase the probability that managers will take their performance management responsibilities seriously. They also make it easier for managers to deliver honest but negative performance appraisals since they will walk into the appraisal discussion knowing that the accuracy of a low rating has been confirmed by their peers. They're a good idea.

Participating in a Calibration Session

The manager walking into her first calibration session is probably a bit nervous. Up until now, her performance appraisal ratings for her troops were shared only with her boss and maybe HR before becoming official. Now they will be posted for a group of her peers to review, and she'll be called upon to explain her thinking behind each of her ratings. Not only is the nervousness understandable, but so is her perception that her job in this meeting is to go to bat for her people and vigorously defend the ratings—particularly the high ones—that she's planning to award.

That perception is a mistake. The manager's role in a calibration session is *not* to defend her ratings or "go to bat" for her people. Her job is to explain her rationale for those ratings, listen carefully to the input from her colleagues, and expand her understanding of the performance of her subordinates through learning from the experiences of others who have worked with them. Then if she sees that a rating she has planned is higher or lower than the rating most of her colleagues would award for the same level of performance, she can adjust that rating up or down to make it consistent department-wide.

Voting is inappropriate, as are back-room coalitions and mutual back-scratching agreements ("I'll support your giving Harry a high rating if you'll do the same for me with Jane"). What's required is managerial maturity and the wisdom to profit from the experience of others. It's particularly helpful if the manager of the supervisors who are participating in a calibration session is also present as an active participant. Not only can the manager add additional insights and share his own experiences with the person whose performance is under review, but his presence also makes coalition behaviors less likely to develop. Finally, by participating in a calibration session, the manager gets insights that would not be available in any other way into the degree that supervisors know their people and are willing to work toward a right answer.

Depending on the number of people whose performance appraisal ratings will be calibrated, the meeting usually runs between one and a half to three hours. An ideal configuration is four to six supervisors in the meeting, each of whom has four to six subordinates. That means between sixteen and thirty-six people will be discussed, a workable number. More than this and not everyone will get sufficient airtime; fewer people won't provide a large enough database for comparison.

An effective, low-tech approach to post ratings is to use sticky notes on flipcharts—one sticky note per individual and one flipchart for each level in the rating scale. Once all the ratings have been posted, the best way to begin the discussion is with the outliers, the people who have been rated 1 or 5. After their ratings have been confirmed or adjusted, then shift to the people whose sticky notes are close to the border between two rating levels. They're the prime candidates for exploring whether the correct rating has been assigned. Finally, review those whose sticky notes are centered in each flipchart. If there's not enough time for a full discussion of everyone, the most important and most challenging ratings will still have been carefully reviewed.

A vital rule for participating in a calibration session is that what's said in the room stays in the room. This means, first, that comments about an individual are confidential. They should only be shared anonymously with the individual during the course of the performance appraisal discussion, and then only if additional support to justify the accuracy of the rating is necessary. More important, the manager needs to take personal responsibility for the rating, and not shift the blame for the appraisal rating onto the calibration group. ("Originally I rated you higher, George, but my colleagues in the calibration session forced me to lower my rating...") That only breeds employee contempt for the supervisor and confirms that the supervisor is nothing more than a powerless pawn in the department.

Reviewer Requirements

The "reviewer requirement" is simply a company policy stating that all performance appraisals and ratings must be reviewed and approved by the appraisal writer's boss before any other action is taken. It's another good idea.

Requiring that appraisals be reviewed and approved in advance by one's boss increases the probability that the appraisal writer will take the task seriously and do it well. The boss can help assure inter-rater reliability by comparing the appraisals written by one supervisor with those written by others. More important, the boss can make sure that all supervisors are setting tough-minded and demanding standards of performance for all the people on their teams. Finally, while legal challenge to performance appraisal is unlikely, being able to demonstrate that a second, higher-level set of eyes reviewed and approved the appraisal makes it even more defensible.

If your organization requires all appraisals to be reviewed one level up before they become official, it's wise to get your appraisals to your manager in plenty of time for him or her to review them. Don't add to your boss's stack of last-minute rush items. In addition, if there are any appraisals that you feel your boss might call into question, attach a brief note explaining your rationale for the rating so your boss knows that you're sensitive to appraisal ratings that might provoke closer scrutiny. In fact, before submitting a performance appraisal with a particularly high rating, it's even wiser to test the waters by talking with your boss about the anticipated rating. His reaction will indicate the amount of justification you'll need to get him to sign off on the rating (or whether it might be better to reconsider the rating you've planned).

If you're the boss in this situation, required to review the appraisals that junior managers have written, your task is not as onerous as it might first appear. Not every appraisal needs intense analysis. In the majority of cases, you'll be fairly familiar with the performance of the individual under review, even though that person doesn't work directly for you. Glance at the final rating and apply the tummy test. If the rating proposed by the employee's immediate supervisor is the same as the one that you'd probably come up with, then just glance through the rest of the appraisal to see that the document looks complete and thoughtfully prepared. For those people you're not particularly familiar with, reading the performance appraisal closely can give you important insights into the strength of talent in your department (and the skills of your subordinate managers in describing and assessing that talent).

Finally, there's nothing wrong with sending what looks like a quickly knocked-off appraisal back to its generator with a note asking, "Is this the best you can do?" The quality of appraisals will dramatically improve once managers discover that their boss is really reviewing them closely.

Preparing for the Appraisal Meeting

There are several aspects to preparing for a performance review beyond simply completing the appraisal form. These range from making the physical arrangements, such as setting a time and place, to ensuring that both you and the employee are mentally prepared for the discussion.

Get Everything Ready

With the performance appraisal approved and ready to be discussed, there are a couple of important elements to arrange in advance of the meeting. The usual recommendations for preparing for the appraisal discussion are well known.

Gather all your materials. In addition to the performance appraisal document itself, you'll want to have performance notes you've made during the course of the year and other support materials close at hand in case they're needed.

Select an appropriate place for the meeting. Your office, with you sitting directly behind your desk, may not be the ideal setting unless you're delivering the performance appraisal of a marginal performer.

Choose a convenient time. It might be a good idea to ask the employee what time would be most convenient for her.

Be cautious about conducting the meeting anywhere outside the normal business setting. One supposed authority on performance appraisal offers some strikingly bad advice: "From personal experience, I believe it's best to complete appraisals at a site other than the workplace. You want to be in a comfortable and relaxed setting and not be bothered by interruptions."[2] Perhaps this author might find that his local pub will provide the recommended "comfortable and relaxed setting," with the only interruption being the bartender's question, "Another round?"

Don't do it. It's a bad place for an appraisal discussion. A performance review is a business meeting. Hold it in a business setting—your office, an available empty office, or a conference room.

If your company, like most, uses a focal-date approach to performance appraisal, there will be a predictable demand on managers' time when appraisal season rolls around. (With the focal-date approach, performance appraisals are all conducted at the same point in the year, instead of staggering them out throughout the year on a calendar or anniversary-date basis.) While the focal-date approach has many advantages over the staggered approach, the biggest problem is that managers are faced with the need to write and discuss all of their subordinates' appraisals within a fairly short period of time.

The solution to this problem is simple: plan ahead. It's no surprise that you're going to have a major administrative burden during, say, the month of November. But you knew this back in January when goals were set and performance plans were constructed. HR departments can make things a bit easier by scheduling just-in-time training and giving you a calendar checklist of everything you need to do and when you need to do it. But the absence of this support is no excuse for shrugging off your responsibilities because of the time demands. Performance appraisal is a core component of your job, just like budgeting. It requires time. Set aside the time you need to do the job well.

Prepare the Individual

Besides the physical preparations, it's helpful to prepare the individual psychologically or intellectually for the appraisal meeting so the person can get maximum benefit from it. You may have asked the individual for a list of his or her accomplishments before writing the appraisal. You may have been required to ask the employee to write a self-appraisal using the company form. But those activities were probably done a few weeks ago. A day or two before the meeting, you can maximize the learning power of the appraisal discussion by sending an e-mail confirming the planned arrangements and asking the individual to reflect a bit on his job and career by considering some questions:

- Has the past year been better or worse for you than previous years in this job?

- What do you consider to be your most important achievements or accomplishments in the past year? (Ask this only if you haven't already asked the individual to prepare this list.)

- What do you most like and dislike about working for this organization?

- What parts of the job do you find most and least interesting?

- What do you consider to be your most important tasks and aims for the upcoming year?

- What can I as your boss or the organization as a whole do to help you be more successful?

The answers to these questions don't need to be written down, just reflected upon. But the simple act of considering them will likely make the individual regard the performance appraisal discussion as a sincere effort toward helping him understand how his contribution is valued and how he can build success, not just as a report-card drill.

One of the main causes of defensive reactions to performance appraisal discussions is that the individual has just been presented with an official document evaluating the quality of his work, which has been reduced to a number on a 1–5 scale. Making things worse, his boss is sitting in front of him while he's speed-reading his way through the document, eager for him to finish so they can begin talking about it. No wonder appraisal discussions are dreaded.

A much more effective approach is to give the individual a copy of the appraisal an hour or two beforehand with the request that he read it and write down any notes or questions he'd like to discuss in the upcoming meeting. This way the employee can have his immediate emotional reaction—positive or negative—in private. He can then go through the appraisal document a second or third time, more coolly considering what has been written and getting ready for a good business discussion.

How Much Time to Allot

There's no rule for how long a performance appraisal discussion should last. With an employee who has worked for the manager for several years in the same position and whose performance is as solid as it has always been, the evaluation can probably be conducted in half an hour of meaningful discussion. On average, setting aside forty-five to sixty minutes is a good time frame. But try to make sure that neither you nor the employee will be facing a rigid ending time, in case the discussion generates numerous valuable insights and perceptions for both parties. You can agree to stop and pick up the discussion later if the clock forces the meeting's termination, but the subsequent meeting rarely has the power of the first one because of the loss of context.

Err on the side of allowing too much time. These discussions differ from most meetings because of the high stakes involved.

The individual's income, self-esteem, and career opportunities are in the balance. And the manager is performing the very delicate task of standing in judgment of an individual in a way that will enhance (or at least not damage) their future relationship.

But managers don't have unlimited time and neither do their staffers. Many employees aren't accustomed to the rigorous personal discussions that a performance review involves. They can become bored, distracted, or overwhelmed if the discussion lasts too long.[3]

The higher the level of the individual, the longer the discussion is likely to last, since there are so many areas that require attention. But sixty minutes is about the limit that any two people can take. The better that both the manager and the individual are prepared, the more likely that a rich discussion will be completed before the hour is out.

The Myth of "No Surprises"

Managers are universally advised that there should be no surprises during the course of a performance appraisal discussion and are scolded that, if the employee reacts with surprise to any point the manager makes, the manager hasn't done his coaching job properly during the year. That's another example of well-intentioned but poorly thought-out advice.

There will often be surprises in a performance review. The process of writing a formal performance appraisal will bring to mind some problem areas that the manager wasn't aware of—or didn't realize the magnitude of—until she gave the individual's performance the close scrutiny that the process demands. She's then in the awkward position of either deciding not to mention a piece of important information because she hadn't previously discussed it with the individual, or rushing to discuss it before the meeting for no reason other than to meet the artificial goal of avoiding a surprise during the review discussion.

It's better to recognize that the information is important and therefore must be discussed, even though it only came to light during the construction of the appraisal. The only honorable course is to include the information, even though it will come as a surprise to the individual when he reads the assessment. In bringing it up, tell the simple truth: "James, I'm sorry I didn't discuss this with you earlier in the year, but I only realized the importance of this issue when I was writing your performance appraisal. I bring my concerns to you as soon as I'm aware of them, and in this case now is the time."

Another reason why there will often be surprises during appraisal discussions is the infinite human capacity for denial. The manager may very well have given the person important information and specific coaching during the year, only to be told in the appraisal discussion, "You never told me that." The fact that the manager may be able to prove that he did discuss the problem area with the individual is irrelevant. Every manager has heard the excuses: "I never thought you were serious." "If it was all that important, why didn't you let me know that you felt so strongly? Why did you wait until my performance appraisal to talk to me about this?"

The fact is, the manager didn't wait. He discussed it with the individual several times, at a level of seriousness that he was sure would have gotten the message across. But denial is a well-honed human capability, and it's very likely to show up during the performance review. Put the blame where it belongs: "I'm sorry you didn't understand how important this was when we discussed it during the year. I hope in the future you'll pay closer attention to what I tell you."

Just Before the Meeting

Just before the meeting begins, a useful technique for keeping things on track is to jot down the three things the person has done best over the course of the past year, and the two areas where performance most needs to improve. Limiting the list to three successes and two areas for improvement is enough for the manager to remember and sufficient to make sure that the most important things get discussed. (One manager admitted that she jotted short reminders of these successes and improvement areas on separate sticky notes and put them on her file cabinet, out of view of the employee but where she could see them easily. After conducting dozens of appraisal discussions, she claimed, she'd never been caught.)

Another useful technique is to develop a core message, the single most important takeaway that you want the employee to remember months later. Human beings are limited in the amount of information they can remember, particularly from an hour-long meeting with a high emotional content. Distill down to a sentence the key idea you would want the employee to be able to recall if a month after the review you asked her what she remembered from it.

Preparing for the Appraisal Discussion with a Marginal Employee

If the appraisal you're about to discuss is for a marginal employee—a person whose rating is a 1 or 2 on a 5-level scale— a lot of the suggestions made above need to be disregarded.

You will still get confirmation that the low rating you've assigned is accurate through the calibration session and your review of the appraisal with your boss. In fact, you may get additional examples that will reinforce the low rating you've decided on and suggestions on how to conduct the session.

But don't give the person a copy of the appraisal an hour in advance. You want the employee to get the message directly from you while the two of you are sitting together. Allowing the person an hour to come up with all her counterarguments is only going to make the discussion more difficult. Skip listing the successes the person has had over the year. You need to present a clear, unqualified message that the individual's performance must be corrected immediately and that the change must happen straight away.

The appropriate place for the meeting is your office, with you behind your desk and the employee directly in front of you— the full-power position.

The "convenient time" may well be the end of the day. The blunt nature of the message you're about to deliver may cause a strong emotional reaction, and it may be best for the employee to avoid the embarrassment of trying to resume work as though completely calm while fighting back tears. Even a person who's going to be fired deserves to be treated with dignity. Treating the person compassionately while delivering a tough shape-up-or-ship-out message may preclude inappropriate be-havior or thoughts of a lawsuit.

Finally, schedule the performance appraisal discussion of the marginal performer as one of the last ones that you hold, not one of the first. Don't tell yourself that since this one will be tough, it's best to get it out of the way early. It's not. Conducting performance appraisal discussions effectively is a skill that grows with practice. Get some practice climbing the foothills before you take on the mountain.

Principles to Remember

DO

✓ Ask your boss to review the appraisals you've written.

✓ Review carefully the appraisals your subordinate managers write.

✓ Set aside more time than you think you'll need for the discussion.

DON'T

✓ "Go to bat" for your people if you're participating in a calibration session.

✓ Be concerned if surprises come up during the appraisal discussion.

✓ Wait until the start of the meeting to give good performers a copy of their appraisal.

Chapter 9

Conducting the Appraisal Discussion

K nock, knock. It's three o'clock. Here's George, standing in your doorway.

"Ready?" he asks.

At this point the performance appraisal has been written and approved. You're ready to sit down with George, spending an hour or so with him and each of your other subordinates in their annual reviews.

Performance appraisal is the time when the manager can exercise maximum leverage at redirecting or reinforcing performance. But without a well-thought-through game plan for the appraisal meeting, a supervisor is more likely to leave bruised feelings and misunderstandings than improved performance.

Unfortunately, the performance appraisal form does not suggest a natural order for the discussion. Too often managers assume that the way to conduct the conversation is to discuss the first item on the appraisal form and then let gravity take its course, continuing on down through every item until the final point is reached.

The form provides the *context* for the discussion. The *content* of the discussion—the items to be discussed, the issues that will be stressed and ignored, the sequence in which matters will be addressed, the points to be made—are the manager's decision. Too often the cause of an unsuccessful performance appraisal discussion is that the manager has not planned an appropriate structure for the meeting but has relied on the form to provide the agenda.

The Focus of the Meeting

Performance appraisal discussions are typically structured in one of three ways:

Successes and positives. The focus of the meeting is almost exclusively on the things the individual has done well, with only passing attention devoted to problem areas and improvement needs. The dominant tone of the meeting is celebration.

Areas for improvement and problem solving. In this case the meeting concentrates on identifying areas where the employee needs to improve his performance, or on problems in the individual's performance that must be immediately addressed. The dominant tone is serious but constructive, appropriate to solving problems.

Balanced message. In this case the supervisor reviews the employee's strengths and successes as well as the problem areas that need to be corrected. The manager and the individual discuss both the positives and the negatives of performance, with usually more stress on things that were done well than on areas that need to be shored up. The focus of the meeting is on maintaining the delicate balance between acknowledgment of successes and discussion of needed improvement.

What's the right approach?

To start, one of the three approaches described above is categorically wrong. Regrettably, this is the one that's probably used in at least 90 percent of all performance appraisal discussions—the one that has left a bad taste in the mouths of so many people who have experienced the traditional performance review. That one is the third approach, the *balanced message*.

The balanced-message technique is traditionally the approach that managers are instructed to use for discussing performance appraisals. They're told to start on a positive note, then discuss the unpleasant stuff, then close on an upbeat note acknowledging the employee's contributions followed by a discussion of the employee's plans and goals for the next twelve months.

To structure the balanced message most effectively, managers are taught to use the "feedback sandwich" technique. As one "expert" on performance appraisal explains it: "You can make effective use of the time-proven sandwich approach by describing both strengths and weak areas in need of improvement, followed by compliments. With this method, you provide positive strokes, highlight areas in need of improvement, then end on a positive note. This method allows you to get your message across but does not destroy the morale and incentive of an employee."[1]

This is colossally bad advice.

This balanced-message approach is the reason people hate performance appraisals. Writer Frank Roche tells the story of a high performer's reaction to getting a balanced-message performance appraisal:

> *I was talking to a friend last night about her performance appraisal. She's a superstar, one of those people that companies drool over. Big talent. Dedicated. Gets up in the middle of the night to work on extra projects. That type.*
>
> *So what happened during her performance review? Nothing bad. She got a good rating, but not the top rating. Plus she heard the "seven good things and three things we can work on" approach to performance management. No good.*
>
> *Here's what I know from empirical evidence: Great performers don't need performance reviews. Especially the yucky and typical kind. They have a great distaste for ratings that can't adequately capture what it means to be up at two in the morning working on a project while the rest of the company sleeps. On top of that, they really resent getting a rating that's anywhere near what Joe Average gets.*[2]

The balanced-message approach to conducting appraisal discussions is a time-proven failure and the source of the distaste people feel for performance appraisal. The problem is that there's no single, clear message. The manager tries to maintain her balance walking the middle of the fence, somewhere between celebration and condemnation, saying some nice things and then some bad things and then some nice things again. It is a technique that annoys and demotivates the good performer and cheers and heartens the poor performer—exactly the opposite of the result that a good manager wants from her performance appraisal discussions.

So, if the balanced message fails, which approach actually works?

Concentrating on Strengths

There is valid research that demonstrates that concentrating almost all the attention in a performance appraisal discussion on performance strengths drives high performance. Research conducted by the Corporate Leadership Council analyzed 105 different factors to assess each one's impact on generating high performance. The factors analyzed included various types of training, performance appraisal, incentives, bonuses, and 360-degree feedback. The research team gathered performance data on 19,000 managers and nonsupervisory employees across thirty-four companies, seven industries, and twenty-nine countries to determine what works. Among other things, they found that performance drivers are "remarkably consistent" across workforce segments, industries, and countries. In other words, "what works here works anywhere."[3]

Interestingly, of all 105 performance drivers analyzed and ranked in terms of their effectiveness in driving high performance, two of the top three are factors that managers have enormous leverage over in their performance appraisal discussions. The single most important factor, the study found, is "fairness and accuracy of information feedback," generating a "percentage performance increase" of 39.1 percent. Risk-taking (38.9 percent) was second. The third most powerful factor in driving high performance, at 36.4 percent, was "emphasis in performance reviews on performance strengths."

What was dead last among the 105 factors that the Corporate Leadership Council studied? "Emphasis in appraisals on performance weaknesses." It turns out that instead of turning someone around, focusing on an individual's weaknesses actually reduces performance by 26.9 percent.

The factor that was found to be most important in driving high performance was the fairness and accuracy of the feedback. In third place was the focus on strengths. Also critical was the *timing*—when and how feedback is given. "Immediate feedback to improve job performance" was eighth on the list of 105 factors with a 26.2 percent impact on boosting performance. "Think about it," writes Brad Hall in analyzing the Corporate Leadership Council's study. "If your child does something wrong, do you give immediate performance feedback (No. 8) or do you document the event and wait until the end of the year to revisit it (No. 105)?"[4]

Concentrating on Improvement Needs

An opposite finding argues that in a performance appraisal, as in coaching, the payoff comes not from celebrating successes and strengths, but from clearly identifying areas where improvements must immediately be made. The value of performance appraisal is in its power to confront poor performers and "rotten apples" with an immediate change-or-else message. Stanford professor Robert Sutton summarizes the research:

> *Studies of workplaces suggest that bosses and companies will get more bang for the buck if they focus on eliminating the negative rather than accentuating the positive. Research by Will Felps and his colleagues on "bad apples" is instructive. Felps decided to look at the effects of toxic colleagues on work groups, including what I would call deadbeats ("withholders of effort"), downers (who "express pessimism, anxiety, insecurity, and irritation," a toxic breed of de-energizers), and assholes (who violate "interpersonal norms of respect"). He estimates that a team with just one person in any of these categories suffers a performance disadvantage of 30% to 40% compared to teams that have no bad apples.*
>
> *So, negative interactions (and the bad apples that provoke them) pack a real wallop in relationships at work and elsewhere. They are distracting, emotionally draining, and deflating.*[5]

With the enormous damage that can be done by toxic employees, it's easy to understand the argument for concentrating the appraisal discussion on improvement needs.

Reconciling the Focus on Strengths Versus Weaknesses

Both focusing on strengths, as the Corporate Leadership Council study recommends, and concentrating on getting marginal contributors to immediately correct their behavior have an appropriate part in the performance appraisal discussion. But the two approaches should not be combined. Unlike the balanced message approach, it's best to focus on one message or the other. If any good is going to come out of the performance appraisal discussion, the two should not be blended. Mixed messages don't work.

To understand which approach to take for a specific individual's appraisal discussion, recall that human performance is a function of two variables, behaviors and results. Both of these variables can be plotted on a dual axis chart, with results on the X axis and behaviors on the Y axis, and the quality of performance in both cases plotted from poor to great. This allows us to identify five different positions, based on the quality of the results the individual produces and the behaviors the person engages in.

In figure 9-1, two of the positions represent effective performers, by far the majority of people in any organization:

Stars. Stars are the people who produce both impressive results and admirable behaviors. These are the people who have earned and deserve to receive a 5 on the company's 5-level rating scale. While their numbers may not be great, stars not only make an outsized contribution to the organization's success but, perhaps equally valuable, serve as role models to everyone else in the company.

Journeymen. These are the good solid performers, the bedrock population of employees in any company. They probably represent two-thirds or more of the workforce. While some of them perform better than others, all of them

FIGURE 9-1

Results/behaviors matrix

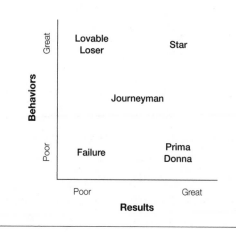

are at least at the Meets Expectations level. Many of them exceed the manager's expectations in one or more areas. Earning the 3 and 4 ratings on the appraisal rating scale, they are the Steady Eddies, the successful strong contributors who form the backbone of any company.

While the overwhelming majority of people in any organization will fall into the Star and Journeyman classifications, there are three other positions in the results/behaviors matrix.

Failures. This group tends to be easy to identify. They fail in both achieving acceptable results and displaying appropriate behaviors.

Lovable Losers. While the people in this group exhibit admirable behaviors, they don't accomplish very much.

Moreover, their failure to produce acceptable results leads others—though they may thoroughly enjoy the Losers' company—to resist having them assigned to their work teams.

Prima Donnas. The Wikipedia definition of *prima donna* characterizes this group perfectly:

Originally used in opera or Commedia dell'arte companies, "prima donna" is Italian for "first lady." The term was used to designate the leading female singer in the opera company, the person to whom the prime roles would be given. Legendarily, these "prima donnas" were often regarded as egotistical, unreasonable, and irritable, with a rather high opinion of themselves not shared by others. Today the term has become a mainstream word outside of opera to often describe a vain, undisciplined, egotistical, obnoxious or temperamental person who finds it difficult to work under direction or as part of a team.[6]

The Failures are not particularly difficult for managers to deal with at performance appraisal time—if the Failures even make it to that point. They are prime candidates for removal as soon as their failure to both act appropriately and deliver required results is recognized. If they're still around at appraisal time, it's not hard to warn them that termination is on the horizon.

Lovable Losers are more difficult to confront—we love them. Whether consciously or not, they rely on their excellent interpersonal skills to mask the fact that they're not producing much. It seems almost cruel to confront them with the fact that the job isn't getting done, they're not bringing home the bacon, they're not showing us the money.

Prima Donnas are the most difficult to deal with, because they are delivering the goods. But they're doing it in a way that demeans and demoralizes the people around them. The most familiar example is the gifted but prickly IT tech who, no matter how badly you've screwed up your computer and no matter how many viruses and how much malware you've allowed to sneak into it, is able with his computer voodoo to get your system up and running better than new in less than an hour. But you'll put up with a sluggish computer for months rather than call him because the guy is such a jerk. He belittles you for letting your computer get into this condition and makes you feel small. But he gets the job done. And it's hard to tell someone who gets the job done that his performance is unacceptable, not because his results aren't outstanding but because he's toxic and demoralizing to all those who have to work with him. People who are undisciplined, irritable, egotistical, obnoxious, and temperamental can and should be done away with. The performance appraisal discussion is the right place to put them on notice that termination will result in spite of their excellent results if their prima donna ways are not immediately replaced with decent behavior.

Performance Appraisal Discussions with Stars and Journeymen

The balanced message technique would have the manager emphasize the employee's performance strengths while also bringing up a smaller number of improvement needs, and then conclude the performance appraisal discussion with some final plastic applause. That approach has consistently failed.

Instead, with Stars and Journeymen, focus almost exclusively on the recognition and celebration of success. Finish the preliminary chatter about the amount of time scheduled for the meeting, the importance that you place on performance appraisal, and the acknowledgment that these meetings are always a little awkward. Then thank the employee for his contributions, granting that you probably haven't said "Thank you" as often as the employee's performance warranted. Say, "Before we progress too much further I want to say thank you for the job you do. I probably don't say it enough, but thank you." That's a particularly effective opening for the meaty portion of the performance appraisal discussion, since not only is the statement true, it is also likely to cause the individual to sit up and listen.[7] A statement like this will lower the employee's guard and reduce the defensiveness that always accompanies a performance review.

From there, move to talking about specific examples in the appraisal document where the employee's strengths and successes were most apparent and your acknowledgment is most appropriate. Doing so will get the two of you into the form, driven not by gravity (starting with the first item and working your way to the last), but by starting with the most important contributions the individual has made and then moving to her most noteworthy strengths.

If you open the conversation in a highly positive and focused way, concentrating on describing the employee's strengths and achievements, this should result in a highly motivating and energizing conversation for the employee. Focus on what the employee did that was good—the results the person achieved and the behaviors that led to success and need to be continued in the future.

Recognize that the word *but* is the great eraser. No matter how positively you may talk about the individual's performance and how many successes and achievements you mention, the instant the word *but* (or its equally pernicious cousin *however*) leaves your lips, everything you've said up to that point will be negated. So don't say it. Stay focused exclusively on success and your recognition of that success.

Will improvement needs be discussed at all? Probably, but they'll be discussed in the context of the employee's overriding strengths and positive contributions. Put aside areas of weakness for the time being. By making sure that your goal for the conversation is a single-minded focus on success, with sincere acknowledgment of the individual's achievements, strengths, and contributions, you are much more likely to end up energizing and motivating the individual—exactly the goals you want the performance review to achieve.

In addition, by limiting your discussion to strengths and successes, you're likely to provoke the employee into initiating a discussion of the places where in fact targets were missed and where opportunities for performance improvement lie. The odds are good that the employee will bring the conversation around to areas of deficiency or needs for performance improvement simply because you haven't raised them yourself. The difference is that these problem areas will be brought up by the individual in response to your recognition of his success, rather than by you because you feel the need to dwell on some negatives so as to temper a one-sided success story. Top performers are usually the ones who are the most self-critical. The chances of the individual's raising problem areas and being self-critical are much greater if you start by withholding any criticism in your own remarks.

Should We Really Focus Only on Strengths?

My advice to focus your appraisal discussions exclusively on strengths and successes and to leave weaknesses or suggestions for improvement for the employee to bring up (or leave them for a later conversation) directly contradicts conventional wisdom and the way we've always done performance appraisals. But what has doing performance appraisals the way they've always been done produced? The tired balanced-message, sandwich-technique approach has resulted in apathy and resentment about the performance appraisal process from our best performers. With only 5 percent of managers reporting that they are "very satisfied" with their company's performance management process, it's time for a radical change in how performance appraisal discussions are conducted.[8] The research done by the Corporate Leadership Council and other organizations clearly confirms that "emphasis in performance reviews on performance strengths" is one of the highest-impact ways that managers can build performance excellence in their work unit.

At the end of the conversation, Stars and Journeymen need to walk out of your office feeling good. If the employee doesn't feel good, you haven't done your job.

But remember, these are Journeymen and Stars we're talking about. This advice is completely inappropriate for the other three types of performers—the Failures, Lovable Losers, and Prima Donnas.

Performance Appraisal Discussions with Failures, Lovable Losers, and Prima Donnas

With the Star and the Journeyman, the focus of the performance appraisal should be almost exclusively on recognition and sincere congratulations for a job well done, with discussions of improvement needs left for another time. With the poor performer, whether the category is Failure, Lovable Loser, or Prima Donna, the appraisal discussion will be radically different.

Like the discussions with Stars and Journeymen, this conversation will also be one-sided, not balanced. But the focus now will be on the need for an immediate and total turnaround if the person is to remain employed. If strengths are discussed, it should be only to acknowledge that while the employee has demonstrated their existence, these strengths either haven't been deployed for the organization's benefit or have been rendered insignificant because of the severity of the employee's problem areas. If successes are mentioned, the context should be that their impact is overpowered by the magnitude of the person's failings. You don't want people to fixate on the small amount of positive information they hear and fail to understand the core message—that their performance is unacceptable and must immediately be corrected.

While the Star and the Journeyman will be caught off guard by this radical change in the content of their performance reviews, your marginal performers will be even more taken aback.

They're used to getting a conventional sandwich-technique review, where the manager says some nice things before getting into genuine concerns, but then wraps up with some more nice things, all the time hoping that her explanations of problems and needed changes will be heard and heeded.

They won't be. The poor performer will hear only the tiny number of positive comments you make and will take no notice of your long account of problems and improvement needs. He will walk out of the appraisal conversation with the feeling that all must be well since both good stuff and not-so-good stuff, as always, was discussed. But all is not well, and the employee needs to be told that to the exclusion of anything else.

For the first time the marginal employee will encounter a performance appraisal that is unilaterally focused on problems that must be corrected immediately if employment is to continue. He will likely respond by saying that he's always had good appraisals and that his work this year was no worse than at any time in the past. That may well be true, the manager can acknowledge, and admit that the individual may have been done a disservice by not having the facts presented as clearly in the past as they are being presented now. But that doesn't change the fact that the individual's performance in the past year was not at an acceptable level and that immediate and complete correction must occur.

Overcoming the Fear of Confrontation

Even though the number of people who fall into the categories of Failure, Lovable Loser, and Prima Donna is very small, conducting a performance appraisal discussion that deals only with the need for an immediate performance correction will be uncomfortable for many managers. For years they have followed the bankrupt advice that they must wrap positive observations around any criticism to spare the individual's feelings. As children they were told, "Don't say anything if you can't say something nice," and they have continued following this bad advice into their managerial positions. Now these managers are required to confront a member of their team with the news that her performance is unacceptable and that continued employment depends on immediately performing at a fully acceptable level. That's scary.

Fear of confrontation is pretty easy to describe, HR expert Kris Dunn observes. It's when you don't want to tell someone the truth or be direct, especially if you think the news won't be well received or will make someone feel bad about himself.[9]

The world is full of people who suffer from fear of confrontation and avoid situations—like a frank discussion of poor performance—where they must be candid and forthright. The manager thinks that by giving direct feedback that contains negative information, she'll turn someone into an enemy. In an interesting twist, the opposite is often true. In a world full of soft-soapers and truth-dodgers, giving someone good, direct, honest feedback in a professional manner is often the best way to stand out as someone who can be trusted.

The next time you avoid a critical conversation because you are afraid of the possible negative reaction or because you dislike confrontation, Dunn advises, fight through it, give the feedback, and tell the truth. Do it professionally and play to the recipient's vanity. Tell her you thought about avoiding the conversation, but wanted her to have full information and an honest assessment. She deserves that, and even though others may not lay it on the line for her, you will.

Conducting the Discussion with the Marginal Performer

Unlike my earlier advice for meeting with the great majority of people who are doing their jobs at a fully satisfactory level or better, don't give the marginal performer a copy of the appraisal to review in advance. If possible, it's also wise not to ask this employee to create a self-appraisal or to generate a list of accomplishments. When the poor performer writes a list of achievements, it will only reinforce the mistaken perception that all is well. But all is not well, and your job is to make the individual realize this.

When the employee comes into the meeting, you may start with the same preliminary stage-setting as with your Stars and the Journeymen (time frame, acknowledgment of awkwardness). However, you need to get to the point as soon as possible: "I need to tell you that your performance is not acceptable. I want to spend our time together talking about the problems I see and hearing your ideas about what you can do to correct this situation." Notice that the manager has said that he is interested in hearing the individual's ideas for correction, not in "hearing your side of the story" or "hearing your opinion." The employee's opinion is not relevant here.

Once that blunt opening statement has been made, the employee's attention will be riveted. You then explain exactly what the problems are and the fact that these problems must be solved.

Most of the time, people problems and performance deficiencies won't be easy to describe in a quantitative way, as in "The standard was 68 and you achieved only 56." A performance appraisal is a record of the manager's opinion of the quality of the individual's performance. This opinion is based on examples of the employee's performance that the manager has observed over the appraisal period and filtered through his lens of experience with similar people doing similar jobs.

Of course, the employee is going to have a different opinion— most of us believe we're above average. The goal in the performance appraisal discussion is not to gain the employee's agreement. The goal is to gain the employee's understanding. As long as the employee understands how you came up with her evaluation, you've done your job. She may disagree (particularly if you've set the bar high and have tough, demanding standards), but don't waste time trying to convince a person that you're right and she's wrong.

Paul Falcone, vice president of HR for Time Warner Cable and a prolific author on performance management, observes that perception is reality until proven otherwise. The manager's responsibility in a performance appraisal discussion is to raise difficult issues directly in terms of his or her own perception, particularly when the issue being addressed is sensitive and unquantifiable, a function of the manager's judgment based on his observations of the employee's behavior and the impact of that behavior.

Falcone's sensible model recommends that the manager start by stating his precise concern, follow with the examples that generated the manager's perception, then close with a request for the employee's reaction to that perception or with a specific request for change. Following are some narratives from Falcone that illustrate how this discussion might go.

Unacceptable Customer Service

"Pat, your customer service orientation is of serious concern to me at this point:

- You appear to become frustrated when customers ask too many questions.

- You seem to have little patience for customers' 'dumb questions.'

- On occasion, customers have complained about your sarcastic and condescending tone of voice.

    I guess at this point I'm wondering if you're happy here, or if customer service may not be the right career for you."

Weak Critical Thinking Skills

"Vanessa, I have to share with you my concerns that you may be out of your depth in your current role.

- We've discussed the fact that you sometimes fail to draw sound conclusions or recommendations.

- You sometimes give little thought to how your decisions might affect other departments.

- And you don't consistently assess the benefits and consequences of a particular course of action.

    Tell me how you see the situation and whether my impression is somehow off the mark."

Bad Attitude

"Michelle, I'm worried about your behavior and conduct:

- You seem to be angry much of the time—almost as if you're challenging me and others to disagree with you.
- I get the feeling that you have some kind of chip on your shoulder and I don't know why.

I'm wondering if you'd be willing to lighten up your style, create a more inclusive work environment, and certainly heighten your awareness to pick up on social cues and read people more accurately."[10]

Recognize that it may not be possible for the individual to "heighten her awareness to pick up on social cues" and "read people more accurately." But that's what the job demands, and the individual is not providing what is required. The manager has met his responsibility by accurately informing the employee of exactly what his perceptions are, providing the examples that generated the perception, and letting her know what's necessary to continue in the role. Finding a solution to the problem is the employee's responsibility—whether she applies learnings gained from a training program, observes someone who is a master of working comfortably with others, takes Dale Carnegie's ancient advice in *How to Win Friends and Influence People*, or perhaps decides that working in this job for this manager isn't right for her and seeks new employment elsewhere.

The direct confrontation of unacceptable performance in the appraisal discussion will undoubtedly be painful for the poor performer, but it's necessary for the overall good health of the work unit. The resulting change is likely to be appreciated by her coworkers even more than by the manager and the employee's customers; it's the individual's coworkers who probably suffer the most by having to work with an incompetent or arrogant associate. They not only have to get the job done, they have to overcome the negative influence of a toxic colleague.

Resistance and denial are predictable. While you may be confronted with that pushback, there's a good chance that you're simply putting on record what, deep down, the individual already knows. Your assessment is unlikely to be a total surprise. While almost all of us suffer from some degree of self-delusion about our performance (as we also do about our good looks and our athletic ability), almost no one is so completely delusional that he fails to recognize that room for improvement exists. Your job is to make sure the person understands that the room for improvement is much bigger than he realized.

Performance appraisal is hard. And abandoning the shopworn sandwich technique in favor of focusing exclusively on what's most important may well make appraisal discussions of poor performers, at least the first time, even harder. But then they will become easier, because the manager will be simply telling the truth as she sees it, celebrating success in the great majority of cases and demanding complete correction in the few cases where performance is not acceptable. One of the wisest observations about performance appraisal was made to me a few years ago by Phyllis Bleymeyer, then head of performance management for John Deere: "If a manager finishes a performance appraisal discussion and says to himself, 'That wasn't as hard as I thought it might be,' he's probably not done as good a job as he could have." Performance appraisal discussions, where one person stands in judgment of another, will always be difficult.

Dealing with Rating Disappointment

It's the universal human condition to believe that we're better than we really are, and this misjudgment often shows up when people who are fully satisfactory performers are rated as Successful (a 3 on their company's 5-level rating scale) and are not given the 4 or 5 they would have awarded themselves. The manager can eliminate some of these misunderstandings by clearly communicating well in advance of the appraisal discussion the idea that the middle rating represents a fully successful level of performance. Sometimes that message needs to be explained in more detail.

Here's an example of a manager doing a great job of explaining to a recently hired, highly talented engineer what Successful, the middle rating in Acme Industries' performance appraisal system, represents. Robert, the employee, probably raises all of the concerns about getting only the middle rating that a manger is likely to encounter. Pam, his boss, confidently and appropriately deals with each one.

> *Pam:* ... and that's why I rated your performance as Successful.
>
> *Robert:* (*Stunned.*) That's it?
>
> *Pam:* What do you mean?
>
> *Robert:* Successful? That's all?
>
> *Pam:* What do you mean, "That's all"? That's a rating you can be proud of.

Robert: Proud of? You're telling me that I'm in the middle, I'm average, I'm no better or worse than anyone else.

Pam: (*Shuffling papers on her desk to find the ratings definitions.*) Robert, that's not what I'm saying. I'm telling you that you did a good job. Here, let's look at what a Successful rating means.

Robert: Oh, put away that piece of paper. I know what it means. It means I'm average, I'm mediocre, I'm run of the mill.

Pam: That's not true! Look at this. Read this with me and tell me that it doesn't describe almost perfectly the way you performed over the past year.

Robert: I know what it says. And I know what you said. All year long you told me that I'm doing well . . . that I'm doing a great job. And now you call me "Average"!

Pam: Robert, that is simply not true. Yes, I told you that you were doing well. That's what "Successful" means. But there is no relationship between being rated as Successful here at Acme Industries and being "average." Acme has tough standards. We set the bar high here. And you were successful.

Robert: You have to give me this, don't you? I know. Only a small percentage of people can get Highly Successful or Outstanding, so it doesn't matter whether you think I did excellent work. Your hands are tied. You can't do anything.

Pam: (*Says nothing but waits for him to continue.*)

Robert: Isn't that true? The company restricts the number of people who can get a high rating, so it doesn't matter how well I do.

Pam: Robert, I need to be clear again. Yes, we do have distribution guidelines. That's no secret. But no guideline or distribution requirement forced me to come up with any rating, yours or anyone else's. I made this decision completely by myself. I paid close attention to the way you did your job and I evaluated your performance as Successful. (*Pause.*)

(*She continues calmly.*) Robert, I need to tell you two things. It's important that you hear me. One. You did do an excellent job. I am proud of how you performed and you can be proud of how you performed. Two. I read the descriptions of each of our five ratings. I thought hard about which one best described the way you performed your job this year. And the answer—my answer—is that the Successful rating is the right rating. And you can be proud of that, too.

Robert: So what do I need to do? How do I get a Highly Successful or Outstanding rating?

Pam: I can't tell you that. I can't give you a list of specifications and tell you, "Robert, you do these things and you'll get an Outstanding rating." Sorry, can't be done. But I can make a couple of suggestions that may help you. First, look at this with me. (*Hands him Acme's definitions of the company's performance appraisal ratings.*)

We don't have any secrets here. This tells you, tells anyone, just what performance looks like at each of the five levels. Read each one. I think when you read it, you'll realize that Successful is a pretty good description of how you performed over the last year.

Another thing. Look around you. Look at the people you're working with, the ones on the teams you're on. Imagine that you're the manager. Which one would you rate as Outstanding? Now figure out what he or she is doing that makes them outstanding in your eyes. Who are the people you think of as models? What are they doing? Figure it out. You can learn from them.

Robert: Will this hurt me?

Pam: Hurt you? How?

Robert: I won't get as much of a salary increase. I won't be as likely to get promoted as other people.

Pam: Robert, we take compensation very seriously. We make sure that you, and everyone else who does his job at a Successful level, is paid properly. And we make sure that promotions go to the person who's best for the job. (*Pause.*)

Do this. Read the descriptions. Think about what you need to do so that at the end of next year, I won't have any choice but to rate you as Highly Successful or Outstanding. But remember, the bar gets higher every year. I believe that you have the capability. What do you believe?

Robert: I believe I can. But it's disappointing not to get the top rating. I always got the top rating before.

Pam: You didn't work for Acme before. How long have you worked for Acme?

Robert: Fifteen months. This is my first performance review.

Pam: And it's a good review. You've been here a year and a half; you're in a tough, demanding job; there have been roadblocks and obstacles; and you still performed at a Successful level. That's good. Can you do even better next year? I think so. I think you've got the capability. But you've got to show me, and show me in a way that leaves no doubts. I think you can do it. Do you?

Robert: Yes. Yes I can. And thank you for being honest with me.

In this example, the manager referred to the company's definitions of each level of performance on the rating scale. If your organization has such a set of definitions, use them to help people understand what each rating means. If your company doesn't, it's no great loss—those definitions rarely provide a clear understanding of the level of performance that each rating level is supposed to represent.

Employees may develop erroneous expectations from the recognition that good managers routinely give staff members. When managers tell employees "Good job!" the employee may interpret that as "Outstanding performance!" and then expect the Outstanding rating on the appraisal form. But they may forget the manager's "This could have been done better" observation when they're reading the appraisal.

Finally, Pam skillfully avoided the trap of trying to tell Robert what he would have to do in order to get a higher rating. As explained earlier, attempting to predict the future and specify exactly what a person will need to do to get a 4 or a 5 rating is simply not possible. But if managers are clear on what middle-level, fully successful performance looks like, then the exceptions that justify a higher or lower rating will be obvious.

Following Up on Earlier Coaching

Another issue that needs to be addressed in the performance appraisal discussion is the employee's performance following a coaching session by the manager. In chapter 5 we listened in on a coaching session between a manager and an engineer who was having difficulty getting people to accept her as a project manager and follow her direction. That coaching session concluded with the employee's coming up with a plan for learning from a successful colleague.

What happened as a result? That loop needs to be closed in the performance appraisal discussion:

Anne: You rated me Successful . . .

Tom: Yes, I did.

Anne: Well, I'm relieved. I thought that after our midyear discussion, I'd probably end up with a rating of Needs Improvement. In fact, I think you told me then that my work on the quality project was unsatisfactory.

Tom: It was unsatisfactory, Anne. I'm glad that you heard me. But you also heard what I said about the need for significant improvement.

Anne: I sure did. But everything came out OK. Gwen was willing to help me. In fact, she let me sit in on a couple of her team meetings, and then afterward we spent some time talking about the things that she did and the way she ran the meeting. I can't do everything the same way she did it . . . I'm not Gwen . . . but the way she talked to people and held them responsible for meeting the commitments they made was something I hadn't seen before. I didn't know how to do that. Now I do.

Tom: So what exactly did you do?

Anne: Well, after watching a couple of Gwen's sessions I got the quality project team together and we went over exactly where we were, and why that wasn't a very good place. And I was honest about the places where I felt that I hadn't done my job as project leader, like in not getting a replacement the minute Simpson announced he was leaving. By being frank about my mistakes, it kind of gave me permission to talk to everyone on the team about how they also shared the responsibility for where we were.

Tom: (*Nodding.*) And ...

Anne: Well, the big change happened when I asked them how they wanted to be managed. (*Looks at a curious Tom.*) Yeah, I actually asked them what would be the best way for me to be their project manager and make sure they got done what they were responsible for. Daily quick briefings? Leave me alone until I come to you? Check in with me from time to time? They were surprised that I asked them that question, "How would you like me to manage you?"

Tom: And the result?

Anne: You saw the result. We came in on time and on budget. I admit there were some times when I wasn't sure, but the whole thing turned around after you and I had the midyear review and after our discussions over the past few months.

Tom: That's good.

Anne: I'm glad you see me as a successful project manager.

Tom: You were ultimately successful on that one, Anne, but frankly, it was a close call. If I looked at the whole effort, and put as much weight on how you started out as on how you finished up, I would have rated you Needs Improvement.

Anne: Oh. (*Pause.*) Do you really feel that it would have been more honest to rate me as Needs Improvement?

Tom: No. If I felt that was the right rating, that's what you would have gotten. I read the behaviors and descriptions for each level and, looking at the whole year, Successful was right. But you still need to do some work in this area. It's important for your career. We know how good an engineer you are. I need to know how good a manager you can be. If you want to be a manager . . .

Anne: I think I do. I wouldn't have said that at the midyear. Back then I was, "Give me my assignment, leave me alone, I'll deliver good stuff on time." I wasn't sure about being a manager. I feel better about it now, like it really is something I think I can do.

Tom: I think so too. Frankly, I was impressed with the way you sought out Gwen and learned from her. She's busy . . . she wouldn't have spent as much time with you if she didn't feel like anything was coming of it. And that reminds me, there's a project coming up that I'd like the two of you to work on together . . .

In this example the manager listened far more that he talked, using phrases like "So what exactly did you do?" and "And the result?" He was direct about having considered the Needs Improvement rating and took responsibility for his decision on the correct rating level.

Are Performance Appraisals Still of Value?

In this chapter I have recommended that managers abandon the tried-and-not-so-true sandwich technique of surrounding criticism with artificial praise, being careful to combine both the bad and the good in every appraisal discussion. That model has repeatedly failed for the sixty years that performance appraisals as we know them today have been used. The balanced-message approach has generated discomfort on the part of managers, disappointment on the part of recipients, and an overall distaste for the entire process. No wonder performance appraisal is such an easy target for Dilbert cartoons.

But if performance appraisal were really the laughingstock of management practices, as its many critics have made it out to be, it would have been abandoned long ago. If it's so dreadful and demoralizing and worthless, why hasn't performance appraisal been cast on the ash heap of failed managerial techniques?

The reason is that performance appraisal serves an irreplaceable function. It gives us the information needed to make wise compensation decisions, deciding who will get a big raise and who will get nothing at all. It lets us know whether we have excellent candidates ready and waiting for promotion, or whether we must go outside to get the talent we need.

It tells us who our best performers are, the ones who are outstanding in their present positions with the potential to take on more demanding roles. It lets us know who our worst performers are and helps us figure out what we need to do about them. Salvage them? Cut them loose?

Most important, it gives us the mechanism to answer the two questions that every individual in the enterprise asks: What do you expect of me? How am I doing at meeting your expectations?

But we can't give honest and ethical answers if we're constrained by an artificial requirement that we balance the bad with the good, criticisms with compliments. We can't be honest with people if we are required to base our appraisals only on that which can be empirically proven and not on our perceptions. It's disingenuous to limit our discussions only to those behaviors that the employee can change, regardless of whether the job may demand a different set than the individual can provide.

Performance appraisal discussions are among the most difficult transactions that people ever engage in. There is an enormous amount at stake. By focusing only on what is of primary importance—whether it is congratulating a Star or a Journeyman for having a successful year or bluntly advising a Failure, a Lovable Loser, or a Prima Donna that he is an unacceptable performer at risk of discharge—these discussions will be easier for the manager delivering the message and more instructive for the individual receiving it. Performance appraisal discussions will then be seen as some of the most productive and valuable in an individual's entire career.

Principles to Remember

DO

✓ Concentrate your appraisal discussion on either celebrating success or demanding change—not both.

✓ Let your Journeymen and Stars bring up areas for improvement—don't do it yourself.

✓ Recognize that most people believe they are better than they really are and ratings disappointment will be common.

DON'T

✓ Rely on the appraisal form to set the agenda for the meeting.

✓ Pay attention to the hackneyed advice that insists that you cover both strengths and weaknesses in every appraisal discussion.

✓ Let Failures, Lovable Losers, or Prima Donnas think that their few successes outweigh their many shortcomings.

Chapter **10**

Hot-Button Issues

With the conclusion of the performance appraisal discussion—including the employee's signing the appraisal form to indicate that he has reviewed it—and scheduling a performance planning meeting to set goals and discuss any changes in key job responsibilities and competencies for the next year, the performance appraisal process is completed.

However, in almost every organization there is some linkage between the performance appraisal system and the compensation system. Therefore, the manager will need to make recommendations (or a final decision) on whether to award the individual a merit increase and, if so, just how much that increase should be.

Finally, the performance appraisal may have confirmed—or revealed—that the quality of the individual's performance is, in fact, beyond coaching's ability to produce the needed change. In this case termination is the appropriate next step.

These tasks—handling compensation and terminating those few individuals whose membership in the organization can't be justified—are "performance management" processes that managers are responsible for in addition to the requirements of the conventional performance appraisal system.

Compensation

Just how important is compensation in influencing individual performance? Not all that much, it turns out. The Corporate Leadership Council study of the effectiveness of 105 performance drivers discussed in chapter 9 included compensation among the factors that were examined. Compensation, it turns out, has only a small impact on performance. Base pay adjustments improve performance by 3.8 percent while annual bonuses raise performance by only 2 percent.[1]

Why does pay have such a small impact on performance? The reason is that the rewards are just too far away from the activity that generates them. The council report argues that incentives are more likely to attract and retain employees than they are to drive performance. But while other factors have a greater impact in influencing day-to-day performance than the end-of-year merit increase, a common feature of almost every company's performance appraisal process (except for public sector, time-in-grade step-system procedures) is a salary increase that is linked to the individual's performance rating.

The amount of money that people receive in their annual merit increase will vary by the organization's compensation philosophy, by its ability to fund merit increases, and by the state of the economy. But there's a general consistency across organizations and over time in what is paid out in merit increases. In flush times, the merit increase budget will range from 2 to 6 percent of payroll.

There's also a general consistency in the belief that people with higher ratings should get bigger increases than those in the middle, and that those with the lowest rating should get little or nothing. In most organizations, people with low ratings—those whose performance has earned a 1 or a 2 on a 5-level rating scale—can expect to get an increase of zero to $1\frac{1}{2}$ percent. Middle performers, the great majority, in most years can anticipate a raise of 2 to $3\frac{1}{2}$ percent. Top performers, the crowd getting the ratings of 4 and 5, can look forward to a merit increase of 4 to 5 percent.

While the absolute difference in dollars between the merit increase awarded to a top performer and that given to a mid-level performer may not be enough to buy dinner for a family of four at McDonald's, differentiating between the two groups can have a real impact on the top performer's feeling of being appropriately recognized for her contributions. "I'm pleased to tell you that in your next paycheck you'll see an increase of 2.7 percent," the manager might say to the person who generated the best results over the past year. The disappointed look on her face will probably disappear quickly when the manager continues by saying, "And you need to know that even though it may not seem like all that much, it's the highest salary increase that anyone in the department got."

Differentiation is always possible, regardless of the amount of money available for salary increases. Unless that amount is zero, managers can always distribute the dollars available, however few, so that those who have done the best get the most. A few years ago the City of Dallas ended the year with enough money to fund an overall increase of 2 percent of salary budget for merit increases. City Manager Mary Suhm gathered all of her direct reports and their direct reports for a management meeting where she spelled out her expectations that managers would use the city's performance appraisal process to give people straight feedback on the quality of their performance and then allocate increases so that those with top ratings got the most, even though there wasn't all that much money to go around. She gave the troops their marching orders: "I want you to manage to a budget of 2 percent, and I want to see differentiation." Everybody got the message and each department came in both well-differentiated and on budget.

The manager's preferences about how to award salary increases will of course be constrained by the company's policies. Most organizations have fairly rigid compensation procedures or guidelines. Compensation is an area where managers probably have the least amount of flexibility in bending the rules. If the company mandates that the only change in compensation will be an across-the-board increase, the manager must dance to the tune that the organization plays. But if the manager has even a slight amount of flexibility in deciding whether to award a 2.2 percent raise or a 2.4 percent raise, he can use that flexibility in the organization's best interest by making sure that those who perform the best get the most. In awarding salary increases, the issue isn't how big the pie is. It's how the pieces are sliced.

Approaches to Awarding Raises

One common but counterproductive approach to awarding raises is the "peanut-butter approach." The manager spreads the rewards evenly, so everyone gets a little bit and nobody gets much more than anyone else. The salary pie is divided so that each person gets exactly the same size slice, regardless of how well or poorly they've performed. While managers attempt to excuse this approach on the basis of "fairness," it is a manifestly unfair approach. Top performers resent their poorer-performing colleagues getting the same raise that they do (and, in spite of bans on discussing compensation, the word always gets out), while the sluggards and shirkers are delighted with the outcome. This situation is exactly the opposite of what good management practice recommends. The result is the loss of top talent and the over-retention of bottom dwellers.

There will always be complaints about the unfairness of salary increases. The goal is to make sure that the complaints come from those who are contributing the least, not the most.

The Tragedy of the Commons

Deciding to award an identical increase to each team member is a misguided attempt to assure fairness. Another unwise approach some managers practice is advocating top raises for members of their own group without consideration of the wider body of people in the organization. This shortsighted approach results in a phenomenon called "the tragedy of the commons."

Popularized by the essay of the same name written by Garrett Hardin for *Science*, the tragedy of the commons describes the dilemma that occurs when the short-term interests of individuals are at odds with the long-term interests of the group. The story describes a group of herders who have open access to a common parcel of land on which they can let their cows graze. It is in each herder's interest to put as many cows as possible onto the land, even if the commons is thereby damaged as a result. The herder receives all the benefits from the additional cows, but the damage to the commons is shared by the entire group. Yet if all herders make this individually rational decision, the commons is destroyed and all will suffer.[2]

As Hardin and others point out, the "tragedy" plays itself out in a wide range of modern-day "commons"—beginning (but not ending) with our use of resources such as water, parks and wetlands, fish stocks, and oil. A similar dynamic occurs at work among managers when it comes time to assess their subordinates' performance and hand out merit increases.

As compensation expert Ann Bares explains it:

The actions of many managers would suggest to me that they see their role and their primary objective in the merit pay process to be getting the highest possible increases for each of their reports, however that might be accomplished. If gaming the pay system is the most expedient way to get there, then so be it. The outcome of this behavior is that the ability of the group (the organization) to pay for performance, to differentiate and reward the employees who truly go above and beyond in their roles, is compromised in favor of the individual manager trying to maximize the pay levels of his/her particular group of employees. Performance-based pay ultimately fails.[3]

Addressing this "tragedy" requires more than simply training managers in the nuts and bolts of how the performance management and pay systems work. It requires dealing directly with the definition of what it means to be in a management role. Bares argues that the role of a manager is one of stewardship, of being a good caretaker of the organization's resources—both human and economic. Stewardship involves actively balancing the needs of *both* employees and the organization. Stewardship isn't putting the short-term interests of a manager's direct reports above the longer-term interests of the larger group.

How to Deal with a Raise Request

In many smaller organizations there is no formal compensation policy. There may not even be an HR professional available to consult on merit increases and other pay issues. In these companies, not only is the tragedy of the commons phenomenon more likely to arise, but managers are also more likely to encounter direct requests from their staff members for a raise since there is no specific policy regarding compensation. Without a policy, people assume that if they want a raise, the only way to get one is to ask for it.

Obviously, the best solution to this problem is to develop some kind of compensation policy so that matters of compensation are not handled in a one-off, spur-of-the-moment fashion. But the manager who gets the request may not be in a position to determine what the company's policy will be, particularly if the company is a small owner-operated firm and that manager isn't the owner. Having to say, "You'll have to talk to Mr. Jones about that" lets everyone know that the manager has no power or authority in the really important areas.

Raise-requesters usually offer a combination of reasons why they deserve a pay increase: they've done an outstanding job (this reason is almost always offered regardless of whether it's true), the scope of the job has significantly widened, they're underpaid compared with peers in the office or with the going rate for the job at other organizations, the cost of living has increased since the last salary adjustment, and the universal I-need-more-money motive.

If the manager getting the raise request is the decision maker (the owner of the business, for example, or the managing partner in a small professional firm), the best approach is to thank the person for bringing the matter to his attention together with a promise to get back with an answer by a specific date. From there, he should talk to other people in leadership positions in the company about the whole issue of compensation to see whether the request is a unique event or the tip of an iceberg of compensation grumbles.

It's important to keep in mind the difference between the value of the role that employees perform and their value as individuals. The two are not the same. Every job is worth a given amount and that value is determined by the market, not by the quality of the individual's performance or their need for a greater income. It may be that the value of a particular job has simply been reached, so the refusal to grant a salary increase is not a reflection on the person's worth as an individual but on the value of the job to the company, no matter how well that job may be performed.

If your review of the individual's salary-change request indicates that a pay increase is appropriate (the person is in fact underpaid compared with others in the company who are doing the same job, or it would be difficult for you to replace the individual at anywhere near the salary the raise-requester is currently being paid), don't grant it immediately. If you agree to a salary increase directly following its request, the word will go forth that all the people in this organization are underpaid. The precedent will be set that the way to get a salary increase is simply to ask for it. This will cause you to be held hostage to all the other requests for more money that will immediately follow.

Instead, initiate a second conversation. Explain to the raise-requester that the amount of money paid an individual is a function of two things: the value of the job itself (the amount it will cost to hire a replacement of similar quality) and the quality of the person's job performance. Ask the individual to take the responsibility for examining both how her performance can be improved and how the job can be made more valuable to the organization. What additional duties might she take on? How much extra responsibility is she willing to assume? How much extra effort is she willing to put forth? When these issues have been successfully settled, you can grant the pay increase knowing that both of you have gained from the transaction.

Finally, it's best to separate the discussion about the performance appraisal and the salary change or merit increase by at least a week or more. Yes, there's an additional administrative burden in having to conduct two discussions rather than handling both issues in the same conversation. But each issue is so important that it's beneficial not to mix the two. And if your company's policies dictate that compensation changes must be discussed during the performance appraisal discussion, tell the employee about the compensation change at the *start* of the meeting, not the end. Putting it off to the end is terribly distracting to the individual during the discussion of his performance, when his internal voice keeps shouting, "How much? How much? How much?"

Termination

The performance appraisal may confirm that the individual and the organization are so mismatched that termination is the right answer. Or, during the course of the year, the person's failure to respond sufficiently to the manager's coaching, or his commission of an unacceptable offense, may cause the need to terminate.

Any termination must be carefully planned, with the heavy involvement of HR if this assistance is available. But the responsibility for deciding on the termination, and the delivery of the news, is the job of the manager and not that of the HR rep.

To begin, waste no time with small talk or anything other than the job at hand. In the movie *Jerry Maguire,* Jerry's peer, a sleazy sports agent named Bob Sugar, takes him to lunch with the purpose of firing him. While he's portrayed in the movie as a slimeball, Sugar does one thing right: he gets right to the point. He leads with a clear statement of the bad news he has to deliver: "I'm here to fire you, Jerry," he states within a minute of their sitting down. As HR expert Kris Dunn notes, when you're delivering bad, life-changing news, clarity is your friend. The confusion related to small talk is your enemy.[4]

Here's a brief, step-by-step guide to one of leadership's most unpleasant duties.

1. Say, "Hello, [*name*]. Come in and sit down. I've got some bad news for you." (Note: Communications experts always advise that it's important to set the appropriate tone for the meeting. By starting with the statement, "I've got some bad news" you have eliminated any confusion.)

2. State the reason for the termination in one short sentence: "As you know, [*the reason for the termination.*]"

3. Say, "As a result, it is my duty to let you know that your employment with the company has been terminated as of today." (Note: Use the past tense. Say, "Your employment *has been* terminated," not "*will be* terminated.")

4. Be specific about what will happen next: pay, benefits, unused vacation time, references, outplacement, and so forth.

5. Close by thanking the person for his contributions to the company. (Note: While it may seem odd to thank someone you're terminating for poor performance, almost everyone makes *some* contributions. Ending on a grace note can forestall future problems.)

Be fully prepared to deal with all of the questions that invariably arise at the time the termination is announced—this is one time you won't be able to say, "I'll get back to you on that." Make sure you have answers to questions like these:

- Is today my last day?

- When should I leave?

- Will I receive severance pay? How much?

- Will I receive the bonuses I was eligible for?

- When will I receive my last paycheck?

- Will I be paid for accumulated sick leave or vacation time not taken?

- Am I eligible for unemployment insurance?

- Will you or the company provide employment references? What will you say if you are asked to provide a reference?

- What will my coworkers and clients be told about my termination?

- Will my medical and insurance benefits continue?

- When must I return company property such as a car, cell phone, and keys?

- What happens to my pension, profit sharing, or savings plans?

- Can I continue to use my office or work area to look for a job?

- Can I say goodbye to everyone before I go?

- When can I go back to my work area to get all my personal things?

The termination meeting should be brief—ten to fifteen minutes is usually sufficient. People always want more. You can talk for hours to no benefit. If possible, schedule the termination early in the week so you don't give the person the weekend to brood about it.

In your discussion, don't attempt to justify or defend the decision. Stick to what you know for sure. You don't know, for example, that an employee who has failed a drug screen is a drug user or an addict. What you do know is that his drug screen was positive. Make sure the person has heard the termination news clearly, but avoid any personal attacks, accusations, or justifications ("You should have known . . ."). And certainly don't tell the employee that this is difficult for you. The employee would gladly change places.

Termination is undoubtedly one of the most disliked requirements of being a manager. But the termination of a marginal employee, if handled compassionately and maturely, will only generate relief from those who have had to put up with drones and deadwood, slackers and dedicated free-riders, without being able to take action. And remember—it's not the people you fire who make your life miserable. It's the ones you don't.

Performance Appraisal—A Conclusion

Throughout this book I have stressed that performance appraisal is a combination of many important and difficult processes. These include setting goals, identifying key job responsibilities, and determining the important behaviors and competencies that organizations expect their members to display. The performance appraisal process expects managers to coach their people so that they are able to do their jobs even better. Performance appraisal requires managers to evaluate how well a person has performed, provide that evaluation on an appraisal form with an accompanying rating, and then discuss that appraisal with the individual. It may involve dealing with compensation issues and terminating marginal performers.

Performance appraisal is a big job. It is a duty that is assigned only to people in leadership positions in the organization. The person who does a performance appraisal is entrusted with the responsibility of standing in judgment of another and rendering his opinion of how well that person has performed. This is a job that requires not merely skill, but also maturity, wisdom, and trustworthiness.

By applying the skills and knowledge that I've given you in this book, combined with some wisdom, good judgment, and courage, performance appraisal can be the most positive force available to assure organizational health and job success. Done right, the performance appraisal process answers the two questions that every person who works in the organization asks: What do you expect of me? How am I doing at meeting your expectations?

Principles to Remember

DO

- ✓ Differentiate in awarding merit increases, even if the actual dollar amount is minimal.

- ✓ Ask a raise-requester to provide you with justification for a salary increase, even when you know it's warranted.

- ✓ Make sure you're prepared to answer any question that might arise—*any* question—during a termination meeting.

DON'T

- ✓ Fall into the peanut-butter trap in determining compensation changes.

- ✓ Argue for high raises for your people at the expense of others in the company.

- ✓ Fail to terminate those who are drones and deadwood.

Notes

Chapter 1

1. *Hedrick v. Western Reserve Care System, et al.* Appeal from the United States District Court for the Northern District of Ohio at Cleveland, no. 99-00630: "As we have oft times repeated, 'it is inappropriate for the judiciary to substitute its judgment for that of management.'" *Smith v. Leggett Wire Co.* (220 F.3d 752, 763 (6th Cir. 2000)); see *Krenik v. County of Le Sueur* (47 F.3d 953, 960 (8th Cir. 1995)), which held that federal courts do not sit as a "super-personnel department"; see also *Elrod v. Sears, Roebuck & Co.* (939 F.2d 1466, 1470 (11th Cir. 1991)), in which the finding was the same: "Rather, our inquiry is limited to whether the employer gave an honest explanation of its behavior." *Harvey v. Anheuser-Busch, Inc.* (38 F.3d 968, 973 (8th Cir. 1994)), quoting *Elrod*; see *Simms v. Oklahoma ex rel. Dep't of Mental Health and Substance Abuse Servs.* (165 F.3d 1321, 1330 (10th Cir. 1999)): "Our role is to prevent unlawful hiring practices, not to act as a 'super personnel department' that second guesses employers' business judgments." Also, "We do not sit as a 'super-personnel department' weighing the wisdom of a promotion decision, but are concerned only with whether the employer's explanation for its action was honest," from *O'Regan v. Arbitration Forums, Inc.* (246 F.3d 975, 984 (7th Cir. 2001)).

2. Edward E. Lawler III and Michael McDermott, "Common Performance Management Practices," *WorldatWork Journal* 12, no. 2 (2003).

3. Bersin & Associates, "High Impact Performance Management" study results, August 2008 (n = 716).

4. Steven E. Scullen, Paul K. Bergey, and Lynda Aiman-Smith, "Forced Distribution Rating Systems and the Improvement of Workforce Potential: A Baseline Simulation," *Personnel Psychology* 58 (2005): 1–32.

Chapter 2

1. Lawrence Tabak, "If Your Goal Is Success, Don't Consult These Gurus," *Fast Company*, December 1996.

2. Edwin A. Locke and Gary P. Latham, "Building a Practically Useful Theory of Goal Setting and Task Motivation: A 35-Year Odyssey," *American Psychologist* 57, no. 9 (2002): 705–717.

3. Lisa D. Ordóñez, Maurice E. Schweitker, Adam D. Galinsky, and Max H. Bazerman, "Goals Gone Wild: The Systematic Side Effects of Over-Prescribing Goal Setting," *Academy of Management Perspectives* 23, no. 1 (February 2009).

4. The video can be seen at http://www.youtube.com/watch?v=vJG698U2Mvo.

5. Ordóñez, Schweitker, Galinsky, and Bazerman, "Goals Gone Wild."

6. Ibid.

7. Ibid.

8. Fred Nickols, "The Goals Grid: A Tool for Clarifying Goals and Objectives," http://www.nickols.us/strategic_planning_tool.pdf.

9. Locke and Latham, "Building a Practically Useful Theory of Goal Setting and Task Motivation."

10. Kris Dunn, "Job Description Syndrome and the Case for Fewer Goals . . . ," *The HR Capitalist* (blog), May 20, 2010, http://www.hrcapitalist.com/2010/05/job-description-syndrome-and-the-case-for-fewer-goals.html.

11. Ordóñez, Schweitker, Galinsky, and Bazerman, "Goals Gone Wild."

Chapter 3

1. The example of the big rocks and measures of success for the job of mathematician and other jobs was developed by Jack Zigon, *How to Measure Employee Performance*, Version 2.2 (Wallingford, PA: Zigon Performance Group, 1999).

2. The list of questions, together with other perspectives on the development of key job responsibilities, was prepared by consultant Steve Sussman, Organization Training and Consulting, Vashon Island, WA.

Chapter 4

1. Competency list and behavioral indicators were developed by the Competencies Work Group of the New York State Department of Civil Service, Governor's Office of Employee Relations, and are available for public use at https://www.cs.state.ny.us/successionplanning/workgroups/competencies/competencylist.html#contents.

2. Edward J. Cripe and Richard S. Mansfield, "The Value-Added Employee," *Workforce*, 2002, http://www.workforce.com/archive/article/news/ 31-core-competencies-explained.php.

Chapter 5

1. Corporate Leadership Council, 2002 Performance Management Survey.

2. Herman Aguinis, *Performance Management*, 2nd ed. (Upper Saddle River, NJ: Prentice Hall, 2009).

3. F. John Reh, "Employee Coaching: When to Step In," About.com/Management, September 19, 2005, http://management.about.com/od/coaching/a/coach_stepin905.htm.

Chapter 6

1. From a private conversation with the author, September 1995.

2. Dick Grote, *The Complete Guide to Performance Appraisal* (New York: AMACOM Press, 1995), 136–137.

3. "How to Evaluate Employee Performance in 15 Easy Steps," http://www.ehow.com/how_5023348_evaluate-employee-performance-easy-steps.html.

4. Michael Lombardo and Robert Eichinger, *The Leadership Architect Norms and Validity Report* (Minneapolis, MN: Lominger, 2003), http://goliath.ecnext.com/coms2/gi_0199-720322/Knowledge-summary-series-360-degree.html.

5. Justin Kruger and David Dunning, "Unskilled and Unaware of It: How Difficulties in Recognizing One's Own Incompetence Lead to Inflated Self-Assessments," *Journal of Personality and Social Psychology* 77, no. 6 (1999).

6. "Best Workers," *BusinessWeek*, August 20, 2007.

7. Jeffrey Pfeffer, "The Trouble with Performance Reviews," *Bloomberg BusinessWeek*, June 30, 2009, http://www.businessweek.com/managing/content/jun2009/ca20090630_570973.htm.

8. Susan Webber, "Fit vs. Fitness," *The Conference Board Review*, July/August 2007.

Chapter 7

1. Susan Webber, "Fit vs. Fitness," *The Conference Board Review*, July/August 2007.

2. Dalana Brand and Michelle Biro, "Cultivating Talent Through Performance and Recognition: The Whirlpool Approach," *Workspan*, November 2007.

Chapter 8

1. Dick Grote, *Forced Ranking: Making Performance Management Work* (Boston: Harvard Business School Press, 2005).

2. James A. Neal, *The #1 Guide to Performance Appraisals* (Perrysburg, OH: Neal Publications, 2001).

3. Richard Rudman, *Performance Planning and Review* (New South Wales, Australia: Allen & Unwin, 2003).

Chapter 9

1. James A. Neal, *The #1 Guide to Performance Appraisals* (Perrysburg, OH: Neal Publications, 2001).

2. Frank Roche, "Performance Reviews Poo-Pooed by High Performers," April 16, 2008, http://www.knowhr.com/blog/2008/04/16/performance-re views-poo-pooed-by-high-performers/.

3. Brad Hall, "Improving Performance: The Innovators," *The Street*, September 2, 2010, http://www.thestreet.com/story/10819746/improving-perfor mance-the-innovators.html.

4. Ibid.

5. Robert I. Sutton, "Bad Is Stronger Than Good: Evidence-Based Advice for Bosses," *The Conversation* (blog), September 8, 2010, http://blogs.hbr.org/ cs/2010/09/bad_is_stronger_than_good_evid.html.

6. *Prima Donna* definition from Wikipedia, http://en.wikipedia.org/ wiki/Prima_donna.

7. Script developed by Mark Murphy, "Stop Dreading Performance Appraisals," webinar.

8. Corporate Leadership Council, "From Performance Management to Performance Improvement: Leveraging Key Drivers of Individual Performance," 2006, http://www.adm.monash.edu.au/human-resources/performance-develop ment/assets/docs/further-reading/hrlc-line-manager.ppt.

9. Kris Dunn, "Organizational Kryptonite: Fear of Confrontation," *The HR Capitalist* (blog), May 28, 2010, http://www.hrcapitalist.com/2010/05/ organizational-kryptonite-fear-of-confrontation.html.

10. Paul Falcone, "Holding Difficult Appraisal Discussions," AMA webinar, February 15, 2010.

Chapter 10

1. Corporate Leadership Council, "From Performance Management to Performance Improvement: Leveraging Key Drivers of Individual Performance," 2006, http://www.adm.monash.edu.au/human-resources/performance-development/assets/docs/further-reading/hrlc-line-manager.ppt.

2. Garrett Hardin, "The Tragedy of the Commons," *Science* 162, no. 3859 (1968): 1243–1248, http://www.sciencemag.org/site/feature/misc/webfeat/sotp/commons.xhtml.

3. Ann Bares, "The Tragedy of the Commons and Merit Pay," *Compensation Force* (blog), May 21, 2008, http://compforce.typepad.com/compensation_force/2008/05/the-tragedy-of.html.

4. Kris Dunn, "I'm Here to Fire You, Jerry," *The HR Capitalist* (blog), August 4, 2010, http://www.hrcapitalist.com/2010/08/im-here-to-fire-you-jerry.html.

Index

Note: Page numbers followed by an *f* refer to figures; numbers followed by a *t* refer to tables.

Above Standard rating, 118
accomplishments
  employee's list of, 103–104
  on monthly reports, 91–92
achievements
  discussion of, in appraisal
    meetings, 156–157
  employee's list of, 103–104
administrative assistant, example of
  goals for, 30
administrative family of jobs
  competencies of, 60
  example of goals for, 30
advice, as part of coaching, 75
ambition, and quality of
  performance, 98
appraisal discussions
  balanced-message technique in,
    146–147, 147–149, 155, 158
  calibration sessions before, 15, 18,
    130–133
  coaching follow up in, 172–175
  conducting, 145–177
  core message in, 142
  defensive reactions of employees
    to, 138–139
  disappointment of employees in,
    167–171

  e-mail confirmations of plans
    for, 138
  Failures in, 153, 153*f,* 154,
    159–161, 177
  fear of confrontation in, 160–162
  focal-date approach to appraisals
    and, 136–137
  focus of meeting in, 146–149
  giving employees copies of
    appraisal forms before, 139,
    144, 162
  improvement needs discussed
    in, 146, 150–151, 157–158,
    160, 177
  Journeymen in, 152–153, 153*f,*
    155–158, 177
  list of successes and two areas
    for improvement prepared
    before, 142
  Lovable Losers in, 153–154, 153*f,*
    154, 159–161, 177
  marginal employees and, 143–144,
    160, 162–167
  materials needed for, 136
  meeting place for conducting,
    136, 143
  "no surprises" myth and, 56,
    140–142, 144

Acknowledgments

My thanks go to the many people from whom I have learned so much during the thirty years that I have spent concentrating on performance appraisal. Bloggers like Kris Dunn and Ann Bares amaze me with their ability to come up with fresh insights and new ideas every few days. I am indebted to academics like Peter Cappelli and Steven Scullen, and particularly Ed Lawler, whose research and experience have made huge contributions to the field of performance management and my own understanding. Consultants and practitioners like Steve Sussman, Paul Falcone, and Jack Zigon have taught me a great deal.

This book would not have been possible without the support and guidance of Courtney Cashman and Melinda Merino, my editors at the Harvard Business Review Press. Their intelligence, good humor, and editorial skills not only helped make the book better, but made the process of writing it a wonderful experience. Also at Harvard, I owe a debt of thanks to Stephani Finks for designing an attractive and clever book jacket, and to Audra Longert for arranging for translated editions.

Finally, I am indebted to my wife and business partner, Jacqueline, who provided wonderful support, good ideas, and careful editing.

About the Author

Dick Grote is president of Grote Consulting Corporation in Dallas, Texas. He is a frequent speaker at corporate conferences and meetings. He also regularly presents executive overviews of best practices in performance management to senior executives and HR leadership teams.

Dick is the author of the books *Discipline Without Punishment* and *The Complete Guide to Performance Appraisal. Discipline Without Punishment,* now in its second edition, has become a management classic. Paramount Pictures bought the movie rights to *Discipline Without Punishment* and produced the video series "Respect and Responsibility" with Dick as host.

His highly popular book, *The Performance Appraisal Question and Answer Book,* was published by the American Management Association in 2002. His most recent book, *Forced Ranking: Making Performance Management Work,* was published by the Harvard Business School Press in November 2005. His books have been translated into more than a dozen languages, including Russian, Vietnamese, Arabic, and Serbian.

For five years, Dick was a regular commentator on National Public Radio's *Morning Edition.* For twenty years he was adjunct professor of management at the University of Dallas Graduate School of Management. His articles have appeared in *Harvard Business Review* and the *Wall Street Journal*. His biography appears in *Who's Who in America* and Wikipedia.